PHUNNY STUPH

PROOFREADING EXERCISES
WITH A SENSE OF HUMOR

M.S. Samston

Cottonwood Press, Inc.
Fort Collins, Colorado

Requests for special permission should be addressed to:

Cottonwood Press, Inc.
109-B Cameron Drive
Fort Collins, Colorado 80525

E-mail: cottonwood@cottonwoodpress.com
Web: www.cottonwoodpress.com
Phone: 1-800-864-4297
Fax: 970-204-0761

ISBN 978-1-877673-64-1

Printed in the United States of America

Table of Contents

Table of Contents (continued)

● ●

● ●

How to Use this Book

Proofreading exercises can be deadly dull. It's the rare person who enjoys proofreading his or her own work, and proofreading the work of others can be even more boring. *Phunny Stuph* uses jokes and humorous urban legends to at least help with the problem of boredom. As you and your students tackle each exercise, don't forget to enjoy the jokes themselves. Some will bring laughs or smiles. Others will elicit groans or "This is stupid" or even "I don't get it!" comments. That's okay. Students will at least be paying attention—an important first step before you can teach *anything*.

Phunny Stuph helps students sharpen their skills at recognizing and correcting errors in spelling, punctuation, capitalization, sentence structure, and usage. However, it also does much more than that. It provides teaching opportunities.

Teach in small doses

When you and your students encounter an error in a *Phunny Stuph* exercise, you have an opportunity to give a short explanation or mini-lesson. Teaching in short "doses," with frequent repetition, can be much more effective than long lessons on a subject.

Phunny Stuph includes 100 short proofreading exercises to use two or three times a week, if possible. Make a transparency of a lesson, and have it on the overhead as students enter class. (Cover up the "Possible Correction" and "Notes," of course, so that students don't see the answers.) Have students rewrite the exercise, correcting all the errors they can find.

Or photocopy the exercises to pass out to the students. (Again, cover up the "Possible Correction" and "Notes" first.) Allow students to correct errors right on the handout. (They can use the proofreading symbol for paragraphing (¶) to indicate a necessary change in paragraphing.)

An advantage of photocopies is that students don't need to take the time to rewrite an exercise. You can discuss the errors in the exercise and move on. At other times, the overhead may be much more effective, especially with short exercises. You may even want to call on different students to come up to the overhead and try to make corrections themselves.

Don't worry if you haven't covered a topic yet

No teacher is likely to have completed lessons on every kind of error found in *Phunny Stuph*. Students should not be expected to know how to proofread and correct each story perfectly. Present each story as a puzzle to be solved. What, exactly, is wrong with each? Many of the errors will be easy to spot. Many will not. (And, just to keep students on their toes, a couple of exercises have no errors at all.)

When students can't figure out what is wrong, or don't know how to fix what is wrong, give a brief explanation or mini-lesson, and move on. Then, in the next few days, try to present an exercise with a similar kind of problem, to see if students deal with the problem better this time. Repetition throughout the year will reinforce what students learn.

Use the "Notes" section for guidance

The "Notes" section that follows each exercise gives information about some, but not all, of the errors included in a story. Use the notes for quick reference. For example, the "Notes" might point out that a certain exercise is a good one for helping students practice correcting sentence fragments. Or they might point out that all of the spelling errors in a story are errors that a computer spell check program would never catch. Finally, they might indicate a rule or guideline that students should learn, such as "Items in a series should be separated by commas."

You may want to use a *Phunny Stuph* story now and then as a proofreading quiz. Refer to the notes to help you find an exercise that includes only problems you have already reviewed with the students. If there are errors that deal with subjects you haven't covered yet, give extra credit if students can find and correct those errors, too. (Many students will work much harder to answer an extra credit question than a regular test question!)

Remember that errors don't usually occur in neat categories

When students proofread their own work, or the work of others, they aren't likely to find errors that fall neatly into one category or another. A paper is unlikely to include *only* spelling errors, or *only* errors in verb tense. That's why the exercises in *Phunny Stuph* generally involve a mixed-up collection of errors—some subtle, some not-so-subtle. In real life writing, people slip up in many ways. *Phunny Stuph* tries to mirror the kinds of errors students make all the time.

A special note: The exercises in this book take the approach that a quotation should include the words a person actually spoke, even if the person used poor English. Therefore, students are not expected to change the words in a direct quotation. They are, however, expected to correct spelling or punctuation errors.

There is more than one correct "solution" to each exercise

Keep in mind that the "Possible Correction" included after each story is only that—a *possible* correction. In most cases, many other possibilities exist for correcting a story. Part of the value of completing a proofreading exercise is seeing that there is often no single right or wrong way to correct a piece. It is important for students to see that writers have choices and control over their writing.

Alligators

While fishing off the florida coast a tourist capsized his boat. Cuz of his fear of alligators he was afraid to swim ashore. Clinging to the overturned boat he saw a man standing on the shore. He yelled, "are there any alligators around here?"

The man yelled back, "no they haven't been around here for years."

Feeling safe the tourist started swimming calmly toward shore. About halfway there he yelled back at the man on shore. "how did you get rid of the alligators?"

"we didn't do anything," the man called back. "the sharks got them all."

POSSIBLE CORRECTION:

While fishing off the Florida coast, a tourist capsized his boat. Because of his fear of alligators, he was afraid to swim ashore. Clinging to the overturned boat, he saw a man standing on the shore. He yelled, "Are there any alligators around here?"

The man yelled back, "No, they haven't been around here for years."

Feeling safe, the tourist started swimming calmly toward shore. About halfway there, he yelled back at the man on shore. "How did you get rid of the alligators?"

"We didn't do anything," the man called back. "The sharks got them all."

NOTES:
- *Cuz* should be spelled *because.*
- The first word of a sentence in a line of dialogue should be capitalized, just as the first word in any sentence should be capitalized.
- Introductory elements in a sentence should be followed by a comma. (Introductory elements include clauses, phrases, introductory words like *yes, no, oh,* etc. This exercise has a number of them.)

The Gift

Because he had been away on business for a week Bill thought it would be nice to surprise his wife with a little gift. He went to the cosmetics counter, and asked for some perfume. The clerk showed him a bottle that costed $50.00. "Thats a bit to expensive," said Bill. The clerk returned with a bottle for $30.00. "Thats still more than I wanted to pay," said Bill. The clerk sighed, and returned with a tiny $15.00 bottle. Bill still wasn't happy. "What I mean," he said, "is that Id like to see something real cheap."
The clerk handed him a mirror.

POSSIBLE CORRECTION:

Because he had been away on business for a week, Bill thought it would be nice to surprise his wife with a little gift. He went to the cosmetics counter and asked for some perfume. The clerk showed him a bottle that cost $50.00.

"That's a bit too expensive," said Bill. The clerk returned with a bottle for $30.00. "That's still more than I wanted to pay," said Bill. The clerk sighed and returned with a tiny $15.00 bottle. Bill still wasn't happy. "What I mean," he said, "is that I'd like to see something real cheap."

The clerk handed him a mirror.

NOTES:

- Commas are *not* used to separate a compound verb. (He *went* to the cosmetics counter and *asked* for some perfume. If the noun had been repeated, the comma would be necessary, as in this version: He went to the cosmetics counter, and *he asked* for some perfume.)
- *Costed* is not correct. The word should be *cost*.
- An apostrophe is needed to show letters left out in a contraction (*that's*).
- *Too* expensive is correct. (A hint: Point out that *to*–with one *o*–is usually pronounced "tuh." Would they say "tuh expensive"? No. Therefore *too* is correct. If they try plugging in the "tuh" sound when puzzling over which form to use, they will usually choose correctly.)
- When writing dialogue, start a new paragraph with each change of speakers.

Free Haircut

A man and a little boy went into a barbershop together. The man received the full treatment—shave shampoo manicure haircut etc. Then he placed the little boy in the chair. "I'm going to run out and buy a newspaper some breath mints and a cup of coffee," he said. "I'll be right back."

By the time the barber was finished with the boy's haircut the man still hadn't returned. "Looks like your daddys forgotten all about you," joked the barber. "Oh that wasn't my daddy," said the boy. "He just walked up to me took me by the hand and said, "Come on, son. We're going to get a free haircut!"

POSSIBLE CORRECTION:

A man and a little boy went into a barbershop together. The man received the full treatment—shave, shampoo, manicure, haircut, etc. Then he placed the little boy in the chair. "I'm going to run out and buy a newspaper, some breath mints, and a cup of coffee," he said. "I'll be right back."

By the time the barber was finished with the boy's haircut, the man still hadn't returned. "Looks like your daddy's forgotten all about you," joked the barber.

"Oh, that wasn't my daddy," said the boy. "He just walked up to me, took me by the hand and said, 'Come on, son. We're going to get a free haircut!'"

NOTES:
- This is a good exercise to review the need to use commas to separate items in a series.
- An apostrophe is needed to show letters left out in a contraction. *Daddy's* in "Looks like your daddy's forgotten all about you," is a contraction of *daddy has*.
- Introductory words like *yes, no, well, oh,* etc. should be followed by a comma.
- When writing dialogue, start a new paragraph with each change of speakers.

Grocery Game

A young man was picking up a few things at the supermarket when he noticed an old woman following him around. He ignored her and continued shopping. When he was approaching the checkout line, she slipped in front of him.

"Excuse me," she said. "I know you noticed me staring at you, and I'm sorry if I made you feel uncomfortable. It's just that you look so much like my son, who died last month." "Oh, I'm so sorry," said the young man. "Is there anything I can do for you?" "As a matter of fact, there is," she answered. "It may sound silly, but would you just say, 'Goodbye, Mother,' when I'm leaving? It would make me feel so much better to hear those words again. "Of course, said the young man. As the old woman took her groceries and left, he called out, "Goodbye, Mother!" Then the clerk rang up his bread, milk, and eggs. The young man was shocked to see that his total was $132.50. "Wait a minute," he said. "How can I owe that much? I only bought three items!" "Your mother said you would pay for her," said the clerk.

POSSIBLE CORRECTION:

A young man was picking up a few things at the supermarket when he noticed an old woman following him around. He ignored her and continued shopping. When he was approaching the check-out line, she slipped in front of him.

"Excuse me," she said. "I know you noticed me staring at you, and I'm sorry if I made you feel uncomfortable. It's just that you look so much like my son, who died last month."

"Oh, I'm so sorry," said the young man. "Is there anything I can do for you?"

"As a matter of fact, there is," she answered. "It may sound silly, but would you just say, 'Goodbye, Mother,' when I'm leaving? It would make me feel so much better to hear those words again."

"Of course," said the young man. As the old woman took her groceries and left, he called out, "Goodbye, Mother!"

Then the clerk rang up his bread, milk, and eggs. The young man was shocked to see that his total was $132.50. "Wait a minute," he said. "How can I owe that much? I only bought three items!"

"Your mother said you would pay for her," said the clerk.

NOTES:

This is a good exercise for practice in paragraphing conversations correctly. All the punctuation is correct. Students need only separate the conversation into paragraphs. (When writing dialogue, start a new paragraph with each change of speakers.)

Dead Rooster

A man driveing down a quiet country lane when a rooster strayed out into the road. The man slamming on his breaks but the rooster disapeared under the car. In a cloud of feathers. The man pulling over at the farmhouse. And rang the door bell. A farmer appeared. The man said, "I think I killed your rooster, please allow me to replace him." "Suit yourself," the farmer replied. "you can go join the other chickens that are around the back."

Possible Correction:

A man was driving down a quiet country lane when a rooster strayed out into the road. The man slammed on his brakes, but the rooster disappeared under the car in a cloud of feathers. The man pulled over at the farmhouse and rang the door bell. A farmer appeared. The man said, "I think I killed your rooster. Please allow me to replace him."

"Suit yourself," the farmer replied. "You can go join the other chickens that are around the back."

Notes:
- When a word ends in "e," the "e" is often dropped when adding "ing."
- "Ing" verbs can't stand alone as verbs in a sentence. They need a helping verb like *was, is, has, been,* etc.
- Complete sentences should not be separated with a comma (*I think I killed your rooster, please allow me to replace him*). Use a period or a semicolon instead.

Homework Excuse

Wheres your homework?" asked mrs. Sedillo.

Justin frouned. "My dog ate it, he answered sadly.

Mrs. Sedillo looked at him sternly and said, I've been a teacher for eighteen years, do you really expect me to believe that?

"Its true Mrs. Sedillo, insisted justin. I had to force him, but he ate it!"

POSSIBLE CORRECTION:

"Where's your homework?" asked Mrs. Sedillo.

Justin frowned. "My dog ate it," he answered sadly.

Mrs. Sedillo looked at him sternly and said, "I've been a teacher for eighteen years. Do you really expect me to believe that?"

"It's true, Mrs. Sedillo," insisted Justin. "I had to force him, but he ate it!"

Notes:

- An apostrophe is used to show letters left out in a contraction (*where's*, *it's*).
- Quotation marks come in pairs. If you have them at the beginning of a quotation, you need them at the other end, too.
- A comma should not be used to separate two sentences. Use a period or a semicolon. (*I've been a teacher for eighteen years. Do you really expect me to believe that?*)
- If someone directly addresses someone by name, the name should be set off with commas (*"It's true, Mrs. Sedillo," insisted Justin.*)

Hiccups

A young man waiting in line at the bank. Developed a loud case of hiccups. Got worse and worse. By the time he got to the teller's window, he couldn't hardly talk. Handing the teller his check to cash.

The teller tapping numbers into the computer. In a moment looking up and frowning. "I can't cash your check," she said.

The man was shocked. "Why not?" he asked.

"The computer indicates you do not have sufficient funds to cover this amount," she said. "In fact our records show that your account is overdrawn by more than $5000.00."

"It can't be!" cryed the man. "Youve got to be kidding!"

"Your rite. I am," she smiled. She started counting out his cash. "You will notice that your hiccups are gone, though!"

POSSIBLE CORRECTION:

A young man was waiting in line at the bank when he developed a loud case of hiccups. The hiccups got worse and worse. By the time he got to the teller's window, he could hardly talk as he handed the teller his check to cash.

The teller was tapping numbers into the computer. In a moment, looking up and frowning, she spoke. "I can't cash your check," she said.

The man was shocked. "Why not?" he asked.

"The computer indicates you do not have sufficient funds to cover this amount," she said. "In fact, our records show that your account is overdrawn by more than $5,000.00."

"It can't be!" cried the man. "You've got to be kidding!"

"You're right. I am," she smiled. She started counting out his cash. "You will notice that your hiccups are gone, though!"

NOTES:
- This is a good exercise for practice in eliminating sentence fragments.
- An apostrophe is used to show letters left out in a contraction (*you've*).
- *Couldn't hardly* is not considered correct usage. *Could hardly* is correct.
- *You're* (not *your*) is the correct spelling when you can substitute "You are" in the sentence.

Training the Cat

Bill and Emily. Madigans daughter adopted a stray cat. They were very unhappy when the cat started using the back of their new sofa as a scratching post.

Don't worry, Bill told his wife. I'll have that cat trained in no time.

Emily watched for several days as Bill trained the cat. Whenever the cat scratched the sofa Bill tossed him outdoors to teach him a lesson.

The cat was a quick learner. Until the cat died sixteen years later he scratched the back of the sofa whenever he wanted to go outside.

POSSIBLE CORRECTION:

Bill and Emily Madigan's daughter adopted a stray cat. They were very unhappy when the cat started using the back of their new sofa as a scratching post.

"Don't worry," Bill told his wife. "I'll have that cat trained in no time."

Emily watched for several days as Bill trained the cat. Whenever the cat scratched the sofa, Bill tossed him outdoors to teach him a lesson.

The cat was a quick learner. Until the cat died sixteen years later, he scratched the back of the sofa whenever he wanted to go outside.

NOTES:

- Use an apostrophe to indicate possession or ownership, as in *Bill and Emily Madigan's daughter.* (The Madigans don't really possess or own Emily, but the phrase is still considered to be possessive since she is "their" daughter.)
- A direct quotation must be enclosed in quotation marks. (A direct quotation indicates the exact words spoken by a person.) Dialogue tags like *he said* or *Bill told his wife* are not part of the direct quotation.
- Introductory elements in a sentence should be followed by a comma. (Introductory elements include clauses, phrases, introductory words like *yes, no, oh,* etc. *Whenever the cat scratched the sofa* is an introductory element. So is *Until the cat died sixteen years later.*)

At the End of Her Rope

Little Allison Stimely had just been put to bed for the tenth time that evening. Her Mothers patience was wearing thin. "If I hear you call "Mother" one more time tonight, you will be punished," she warned Allison sternly.

For a while it was quite. Then she heard a tiny voice from the top of the stairs call, "Mrs. stimely? Can I have a drink of water?"

POSSIBLE CORRECTION:

Little Allison Stimely had just been put to bed for the tenth time that evening. Her mother's patience was wearing thin. "If I hear you call 'Mother' one more time tonight, you will be punished," she warned Allison sternly.

For a while, it was quiet. Then she heard a tiny voice from the top of the stairs call, "Mrs. Stimely? Can I have a drink of water?"

NOTES:
- "Mother" is not capitalized unless it is being used instead of the person's name, as a noun of direct address. Therefore, the word should not be capitalized in "her mother's." It *should* remain capitalized in the second instance (*"If I hear you call 'Mother' one more time tonight..."*).
- Possessives require an apostrophe. *Mother's patience* is a possessive. In a sense, *patience* "belongs" to the mother. (Students may need to see a number of examples before they grasp this use of the possessive.)
- When a quotation includes a quotation by someone else, the second quotation has single quotation marks around it. (*"If I hear you call 'Mother' one more time tonight, you will be punished," she warned Allison sternly.*)
- Many students confuse *quiet* and *quite*. (Sometimes it helps to remind them that the "e" is pronounced in *quiet*.)

Kittens

A three-year-old boy went with his dad to see a litter of kittens. When he got home he ran up to his mom and said, with excitement, I saw the kittens, mom! There were two boy kittens and two girl kittens. How did you know? his mother asked. Daddy picked them up and looked underneath, he answered. I think its printed on the bottom.

POSSIBLE CORRECTION:

A three-year-old boy went with his dad to see a litter of kittens. When he got home, he ran up to his mom and said, with excitement, "I saw the kittens, Mom! There were two boy kittens and two girl kittens."

"How did you know?" his mother asked.

"Daddy picked them up and looked underneath," he answered. "I think it's printed on the bottom."

NOTES:

- "Mom" is not capitalized unless it is being used instead of the person's name, as a noun of direct address. Therefore, the word should not be capitalized in "his mom." It *should* remain capitalized in "I saw the kittens, Mom..."
- A direct quotation must be enclosed in quotation marks. (A direct quotation indicates the exact words that were spoken.) Dialogue tags like *his mother asked* or *he answered* are not part of a direct quotation.
- When writing dialogue, start a new paragraph with each change of speakers.
- *It's,* with an apostrophe, is a contraction used for *it is.* Use *it's* instead of *its* if you can substitute the words "it is."

Putting on Shoes

A four-year-old gril was very happy that she had put her shoes on all by herself. Her Mother noticed that the left shoe was on the right foot. She goes, "Honey, you're shoes are on the wrong feet."

The daughter looked up at her Mother and went, "Don't kid me, Mom. Their the only feet I've got!"

POSSIBLE CORRECTION:

A four-year-old girl was very happy that she had put her shoes on all by herself. Her mother noticed that the left shoe was on the right foot. She said, "Honey, your shoes are on the wrong feet."

The daughter looked up at her mother and said, "Don't kid me, Mom. They're the only feet I've got!"

NOTES:
- *Mother* and *mom* are not capitalized unless they are being used instead of the person's name, as a noun of direct address. Therefore, the word should not be capitalized in *her mother*. It *should* remain capitalized when the little girl says, "Don't kid me, Mom."
- *They're* is a contraction of *they are*. Use *they're* when *they are* can be substituted in a sentence.
- Use *you're* only if you can't substitute the words *you are* in a sentence.
- *Said* should replace *go* in *She goes*. It should also replace *went* in the last paragraph.

Grandma's Visit

Little Christopher was so happy to see his grandmother that he ran up and gave her a big hug. "I'm so happy to see you, grandma," He said. Now daddy will have to do that trick he's been promising to do."

His grandmother was curoius. What trick is that, Christopher?"

Christopher said, "I heard daddy tell mommy that he would climb the darn walls if you came to visit us again!

POSSIBLE CORRECTION:

Little Christopher was so happy to see his grandmother that he ran up and gave her a big hug. "I'm so happy to see you, Grandma," he said. "Now Daddy will have to do that trick he's been promising to do."

His grandmother was curious. "What trick is that, Christopher?"

Christopher said, "I heard Daddy tell Mommy that he would climb the darn walls if you came to visit us again!"

NOTES:
- Words like *mother, grandmother, daddy,* etc., are not capitalized unless they are being used instead of the person's name, as a noun of direct address. Therefore, the word is not capitalized in *his grandmother.* It is capitalized in, "I'm so happy to see you, Grandma."
- The first word of dialogue tags like *he said* are not capitalized.
- Quotation marks come in pairs. Use them at the beginning *and* at the end of the quotation.

Piranha

Miss Changs students were writing compositions. One of them asked her how to spell *piranha*.

"well I'm not sure," said Miss Chang. The little boy went to the back of the room to look up the word in the dictionary.

"why are you bothering to look it up" asked another student. "she doesn't know how to spell it anyway."

POSSIBLE CORRECTION:

Miss Chang's students were writing compositions. One of them asked her how to spell *piranha*.

"Well, I'm not sure," said Miss Chang. The little boy went to the back of the room to look up the word in the dictionary.

"Why are you bothering to look it up?" asked another student. "She doesn't know how to spell it anyway."

NOTES:
- Use an apostrophe to indicate possession or ownership, as in *Miss Chang's students*. (Miss Chang doesn't really possess or own her students, but the phrase is still considered to be possessive since they are "her" students.)
- Capitalize the first word of a sentence in a line of dialogue.
- Use a comma after introductory words like *yes, no, oh, well*, etc.
- Use a question mark at the end of a sentence that asks a question.

Fertilizer

A farmer was driving along the road with a load of fertilizer. A little boy who was playing in front of his house saw him. He called out, what have you got in your truck? Fertilizer, answered the farmer. What are you going to do with it? Asked the boy. I'm going to put it on strawberries, answered the farmer. Weird, said the little boy. We put sugar and whipped cream on ours.

> ### POSSIBLE CORRECTION:
>
> A farmer was driving along the road with a load of fertilizer. A little boy who was playing in front of his house saw him. He called out, "What have you got in your truck?"
>
> "Fertilizer," answered the farmer.
>
> "What are you going to do with it?" asked the boy.
>
> "I'm going to put it on strawberries," answered the farmer.
>
> "Weird," said the little boy. "We put sugar and whipped cream on ours."

NOTES:
This is a good exercise for having students paragraph and punctuate dialogue correctly.

Music Notes

Mr. Wheeler the music teacher for the elementary school was giving the first graders their first music lesson. He drew a musical staff on the board and said, "Amelia, come up and write a note on this musical staff."

Amelia went to the board and stood there for a minute. Then she wrote, "Dear aunt emma, I am fine. How are you. Love, Amelia.

POSSIBLE CORRECTION:

Mr. Wheeler, the music teacher for the elementary school, was giving the first graders their first music lesson. He drew a musical staff on the board and said, "Amelia, come up and write a note on this musical staff."

Amelia went to the board and stood there for a minute. Then she wrote, "Dear Aunt Emma, I am fine. How are you? Love, Amelia."

NOTES:

- Use commas around an appositive. An appositive is an interrupting element that breaks the flow of the sentence to give more information about a noun. (Mr. Wheeler, *the music teacher for the elementary school,* was giving the first graders their first music lesson.)
- Capitalize *aunt* and *uncle* if they are used as part of the person's name. (Yes: *Aunt Emma.* No: *my aunt.*)
- Use a question mark at the end of a sentence that asks a question.

Beauty Is in the Eye of the Beholder

A young woman got on the bus with her six-month-old baby. The bus driver said, "Ugh! Thats the ugliest baby that I've ever seen!"

The woman is furious. She walked to the back of the bus and sat down. She turned to the man next to her and said, "That driver just insulted me!"

The man says, "Really? There's no call for that. You go right up there and tell him off."

The woman hesitated.

"Go ahead," he said. "I'll hold your monkey for you."

POSSIBLE CORRECTION:

A young woman got on the bus with her six-month-old baby. The bus driver said, "Ugh! That's the ugliest baby that I've ever seen!"

The woman was furious. She walked to the back of the bus and sat down. She turned to the man next to her and said, "That driver just insulted me!"

The man said, "Really? There's no call for that. You go right up there and tell him off."

The woman hesitated.

"Go ahead," he said. "I'll hold your monkey for you."

NOTES:
- The story switches back and forth between past tense and present tense. It should stick to one or the other. (*The woman* **got** *on the bus. She* **was** *furious. The man* **said**. OR *The woman* **gets** *on the bus. She* **is** *furious. The man* **says**.)
- *That's* needs an apostrophe because it is a contraction used for *That is*.

Psychic Friends

A frog recently called the Psychik Friends Network. His psychik said, "You are going to meet a beautyfull girl who will want to know everything their is to know about you." "Wow, said the frog. "Thats wonderful! Will I meet her at a party, or what?" "No," said the psychik. "Youll meet her next semester in her biology class."

POSSIBLE CORRECTION:

A frog recently called the Psychic Friends Network. His psychic said, "You are going to meet a beautiful girl who will want to know everything there is to know about you."

"Wow!" said the frog. "That's wonderful! Will I meet her at a party, or what?"

"No," said the psychic. "You'll meet her next semester in her biology class."

NOTES:
- *That's* needs an apostrophe because it is a contraction used for *That is.*
- *You'll* needs an apostrophe because it is a contraction used for *you will.*
- When writing dialogue, start a new paragraph with each change of speakers.

The Best Birthday Present

Thanks for the harmonica you gave me," little Michael said to his Uncle several weeks after his birthday. "Its the best present I ever got." "Wonderful," said his Uncle. "Do you know how to play it?" "Oh I don't play it," said Michael. "My Mother gives me a dollar a day not to play it during the day and my Dad gives me five dollars a week not to play it at night.

POSSIBLE CORRECTION:

"Thanks for the harmonica you gave me," little Michael said to his uncle several weeks after his birthday. "It's the best present I ever got."

"Wonderful," said his uncle. "Do you know how to play it?"

"Oh, I don't play it," said Michael. "My mother gives me a dollar a day not to play it during the day, and my dad gives me five dollars a week not to play it at night."

NOTES:
- Capitalize *aunt* and *uncle* if they are used as part of the person's name. Capitalize *Mom* and *Dad* if they are used instead of the person's name. (*Yes: I gave something to Mother. No: My mother gives me a dollar.*)
- *It's* needs an apostrophe because it is a contraction used for *it is*.
- When writing dialogue, start a new paragraph with each change of speakers.
- Use a comma with *and* in a compound sentence. A compound sentence is two complete sentences connected with *and, but, or, for,* or *nor*. (Example: *My mother gives me a dollar a day not to play it during the day, and my dad gives me five dollars a week not to play it at night.*)

Chickens at the Library

One day a pair of chickens walk up to the circulation desk at a public library. They said, "Buk, buk, BUK!" The librarien hesitated but then decided they were asking for three books. She gives them three books, the chickens left.

Around noon, the chickens came back and said, "Buk, buk, BUK!" again. The librarian gives them three more books, the chickens left.

That afternoon the two chickens returned and approached the librarian again. This time they said, "Buk, buk, buk, buk, BUK!" The librarian was annoyed and starting to become suspishus of these chickens. She gives them five books but decided to follow them and find out what was going on.

She follows the chickens. Out of the library. Out of town and to a park. Hid behind a tree. Saw the two chickens throwing the books at a frog in a pond. The frog said, "Rredit, rredit, rredit!"

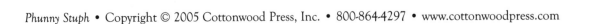

Possible Correction:

One day a pair of chickens walked up to the circulation desk at a public library. They said, "Buk, buk, BUK!" The librarian hesitated but then decided they were asking for three books. She gave them three books, and the chickens left.

Around noon, the chickens came back and said, "Buk, buk, BUK!" again. The librarian gave them three more books, and the chickens left.

That afternoon the two chickens returned and approached the librarian again. This time they said, "Buk, buk, buk, buk, BUK!" The librarian was annoyed and started to become suspicious of these chickens. She gave them five books but decided to follow them and find out what was going on.

She followed the chickens out of the library, out of town and to a park. She hid behind a tree and saw the two chickens throwing the books at a frog in a pond. The frog said, "Rredit, rredit, rredit!"

NOTES:

- This is a good exercise for practicing the use of correct tense. The paragraphs should be in either present tense *or* past tense. (The chickens *walked.* They *said.* She *gave.* OR The chickens *walk.* They *say.* They *give.*)
- A comma should not be used to separate two sentences. Use a period, a semicolon, or a comma with *and, but, or, for* or *nor.* (Example: *She gave them three books, and the chickens left.*)
- The last paragraph has many sentence fragments that need to be corrected.

Queen Size

A little boy went to the store with his grandmother. On the way home, he looked over the things in her bag. Found a package of panty hose and read aloud the words *Queen Size.*

He turned to his grandmother and said, Look Grandma you wear the same size as my mom and dads bed!

Possible Correction:

A little boy went to the store with his grandmother. On the way home, he looked over the things in her bag. He found a package of panty hose and read aloud the words *Queen Size.*

He turned to his grandmother and said, "Look, Grandma! You wear the same size as my mom and dad's bed!"

Notes:

- The phrase "Found a package of panty hose and read aloud the words *Queen Size*" needs a subject. Simply adding *He* at the beginning of the sentence fixes it. Another idea would be to add it to the previous sentence and make a series, like this: "On the way home, he looked over the things in her bag, found a package of panty hose, and read aloud the words *Queen Size.*"
- Nouns of direct address should be set off with commas. (The little boy is directly addressing his grandmother with, "Look, Grandma! You wear the same size as my mom and dad's bed!")
- Use an apostrophe to indicate possession or ownership (*my mom and dad's bed*).

Chess Game

A man went to visit his friend. Astonished to find him playing chess with his dog. Watched the game for a while. "I can hardly believe my eyes," he exclaimed. "Thats the smartest dog I've ever seen." "No hes not so smart," the friend replied. "I've beaten him three games out of five."

POSSIBLE CORRECTION:

A man went to visit his friend. He was astonished to find him playing chess with his dog. He watched the game for a while. "I can hardly believe my eyes!" he exclaimed. "That's the smartest dog I've ever seen!"

"No, he's not so smart," the friend replied. "I've beaten him three games out of five."

NOTES:
- Sentences need subjects. The second and third sentences are sentence fragments because they don't have subjects.
- *That's* is a contraction used for *that is.*
- *He's* is a contraction used for *he is.*
- Since the man is "exclaiming," an exclamation point should be used after his exclamations.
- When writing dialogue, start a new paragraph with each change of speakers.

Mad Cow Disease

Two cows chatting over the fence between their fields. The first cow said, "This mad cow disease is pretty scary. They say it effects you're brain. Its spreading fast, to. I heard it hit some cows down on the Johnson farm."

"I'am not worried," the other cow replied. "It doesn't effect us ducks."

POSSIBLE CORRECTION:

Two cows were chatting over the fence between their fields. The first cow said, "This mad cow disease is pretty scary. They say it affects your brain. It's spreading fast, too. I heard it hit some cows down on the Johnson farm."

"I'm not worried," the other cow replied. "It doesn't affect us ducks."

NOTES:
- *You're* is a contraction of *you are*. Use *you're* when *you are* can be substituted in a sentence.
- *It's* is a contraction of *it is*. Use *it's* (with an apostrophe) only when it substitutes for *it is*.
- Use the spelling *too* to mean *also*.
- *Affect* is a verb. *Effect* is almost always used as a noun. Since a verb is needed in the last sentence, it should be *affect us ducks*. (*Effect* is occasionally used as a verb to mean "bring about" or "cause," as in *effect a change*.)

Feeding the Pigs

A man from the city came to visit a small farm, he saw a farmer feeding pigs in a very strange way. The farmer would lift a pig up to a nearby apple tree, the pig would eat the apples directly off the tree. The farmer would move the pig from one apple to another until the pig was full, then he would start again with another pig.

The man from the city was pretty puzzled, he watched for quiet a while, finally said, "What a strange way to feed pigs! It's a waist of time! You could save a hole lot of time if you just shook the apples off the tree and let the pigs eat them from the ground!" The farmer looked puzzled and replied, "What's time to a pig?"

POSSIBLE CORRECTION:

A man from the city came to visit a small farm. He saw a farmer feeding pigs in a very strange way. The farmer would lift a pig up to a nearby apple tree, and the pig would eat the apples directly off the tree. The farmer would move the pig from one apple to another until the pig was full. Then he would start again with another pig.

The man from the city was pretty puzzled. He watched for quite a while and finally said, "What a strange way to feed pigs! It's a waste of time! You could save a whole lot of time if you just shook the apples off the tree and let the pigs eat them from the ground!"

The farmer looked puzzled and replied, "What's time to a pig?"

NOTES:

- This is a good exercise for correcting run-on sentences (comma splices).
- *Quite* and *quiet* are frequently confused. So are *whole* and *hole* and *waste* and *waist.*
- When writing dialogue, start a new paragraph with each change of speakers.

Sharing

One day, brothers Ed and Tyler went to there Grandmas for diner. As soon as she put a plate of too stakes on the table, Ed quickly piked out the biger stake for himself. Tyler wasn't hapy about that. "When are you going too learn too be polite?" he asked. Ed answered, "If you had the chance too pik first, whitch one would you pick?" "The smaller peice, of course," said Tyler. "What are you whinning about then?" said Ed. "The smaler peice is what you want, rite?"

POSSIBLE CORRECTION:

One day, brothers Ed and Tyler went to their grandma's for dinner. As soon as she put a plate of two steaks on the table, Ed quickly picked out the bigger steak for himself. Tyler wasn't happy about that. "When are you going to learn to be polite?" he asked.

Ed answered, "If you had the chance to pick first, which one would you pick?"

"The smaller piece, of course," said Tyler.

"What are you whining about then?" said Ed. "The smaller piece is what you want, right?"

NOTES:
- This is a good exercise for finding and correcting spelling errors.
- When writing dialogue, start a new paragraph with each change of speakers.

Fussy Customer

A customer was bothering the waiter in a restaurant and first he asked that the air conditioning be turned up cause he was too hot, and then he asked that it be turned down cause he was too cold, and this went on, back and forth, for about an hour, but, surprisingly, the waiter was very patient, and he walked back and forth and never once got angry, and another customer finally asked him why he didn't throw out the fussy guy and the waiter just smiled and said, "I don't really mind, we don't even have an air conditioner."

POSSIBLE CORRECTION:

A customer was bothering the waiter in a restaurant. First, he asked that the air conditioning be turned up because he was too hot. Then he asked that it be turned down because he was too cold. This went on, back and forth, for about an hour.

Surprisingly, the waiter was very patient. He walked back and forth and never once got angry. Another customer finally asked him why he didn't throw out the fussy guy. The waiter just smiled and said, "I don't really mind. We don't even have an air conditioner."

NOTES:
- This item is one long run-on sentence. The challenge is to separate it into shorter, clearer sentences.
- *Cause* should not be substituted for *because*.

Tomatoes

Three tomatoes in a family were walking downtown one day when the little baby tomato started lagging behind and the father tomato walks back to the baby tomato and he stomps on her and he squashes her into a red paste, and then he said, "Ketchup!"

POSSIBLE CORRECTION:

Three tomatoes in a family were walking downtown one day when the little baby tomato started lagging behind. The father tomato walked back to the baby tomato and stomped on her. He squashed her into a red paste. Then he said, "Ketchup!"

NOTES:
- This paragraph is one long run-on sentence. There are a number of ways to correct it.
- The paragraph switches back and forth between past and present tense. It should be written all in past tense OR all in present tense.

The Englishman

A waitress in a New York City Restaurant brought an englishman the soup of the day. The englishmen looked a bit upset. "Good heavens, he said. "What is this?" It's bean soup, said the waitress. "I don't care what it has *been*, he sputtered. What is it now?

POSSIBLE CORRECTION:

A waitress in a New York City restaurant brought an Englishman the soup of the day. The Englishman looked a bit upset. "Good heavens," he said. "What is this?"

"It's bean soup," said the waitress.

"I don't care what it has *been*," the Englishman sputtered. "What is it now?"

NOTES:

- *New York City* is capitalized because it is the name of a city. There is no reason to capitalize *restaurant*. It is not part of the restaurant's name.
- When a person is quoted, his or her exact words should be enclosed by quotation marks.
- When writing dialogue, start a new paragraph with each change of speakers.

The Policeman and the Penguin

One day a Police Officer saw a man walking down the street with a penguin. He told the man he should take the penguin to the Zoo.

"Good idea," the man replied, and off he went.

The next day the Police Officer saw the man again. He still had the penguin with him. "I thought I told you to take the penguin to the Zoo," the Police Officer said.

"I did," answered the man, "and today I'm taking him to the Movies."

POSSIBLE CORRECTION:

One day a police officer saw a man walking down the street with a penguin. He told the man he should take the penguin to the zoo.

"Good idea," the man replied, and off he went.

The next day the police officer saw the man again. He still had the penguin with him. "I thought I told you to take the penguin to the zoo," the police officer said.

"I did," answered the man, "and today I'm taking him to the movies."

NOTES:

- All the errors in this piece involve capitalization. Nouns don't need to be capitalized unless they are the names of *specific* people or places. For example, the word *zoo* isn't capitalized unless it is part of a specific name, like *Denver Zoo*. Similarly, *police officer* should not be capitalized, but *Officer Taylor* should be.

The Announcement

A minister looked out at his congregation one sunday. "I have good news and bad news," he said. "The good news is that we have enough money to pay for are new building program. The bad news is that its still out their in you're pockets."

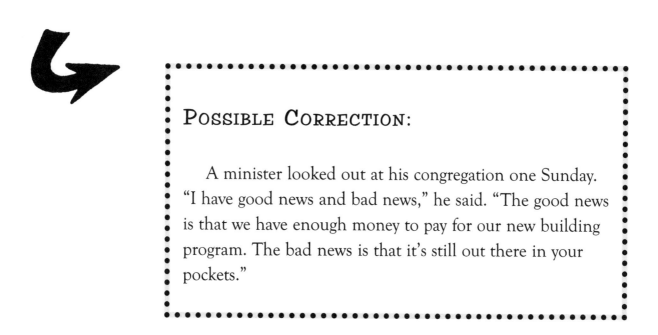

POSSIBLE CORRECTION:

A minister looked out at his congregation one Sunday. "I have good news and bad news," he said. "The good news is that we have enough money to pay for our new building program. The bad news is that it's still out there in your pockets."

NOTES:
- This is a good exercise for practice dealing with those pesky problem words *our* and *are*, *there*, *they're* and *their*, and *you're* and *your*.

Decisions, Decisions

A boy, a preacher, a doctor, a lawyer, and the pilot were on a plane. The pilot came on the intercom and says "Mayday, Mayday! We're going down! There are only four parachutes on the plane. I'm taking one and jumping right now. You guys decide who gets the other three." Then he jumped out of the plane.

The doctor says "I've saved lives my whole life, so I think that I should get one." He grabbed a parachute and jumped out of the plane.

The lawyer said "I'm the smartest man in the world. I've solved over nine dozen cases, so I'm jumping, too. Goodbye!" he jumps out of the plane.

The preacher goes up to the boy and says "I've lived a long and happy life. I know I'm going to heaven, so you take the last prachute and go."

The boy says "No, you grab this one and I'll grab the other one because the smartest man in the world just jumped out of the plane with my backpack!"

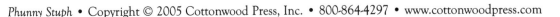

POSSIBLE CORRECTION:

A boy, a preacher, a doctor, a lawyer, and the pilot were on a plane. The pilot came on the intercom and said, "Mayday, Mayday! We're going down! There are only four parachutes on the plane. I'm taking one and jumping right now. You guys decide who gets the other three." Then he jumped out of the plane.

The doctor said, "I've saved lives my whole life, so I think that I should get one." He grabbed a parachute and jumped out of the plane.

The lawyer said, "I'm the smartest man in the world. I've solved over nine dozen cases, so I'm jumping, too. Goodbye!" He jumped out of the plane.

The preacher went up to the boy and said, "I've lived a long and happy life. I know I'm going to heaven, so you take the last parachute and go."

The boy said, "No, you grab this one, and I'll grab the other one because the smartest man in the world just jumped out of the plane with my backpack!"

NOTES:
- The main problem with this piece involves tenses. Writers should stick to present tense, past tense, or future tense. They should *not* move back and forth between tenses in one story.
- Use a comma after dialogue tags like *he said* when used to introduce a quotation. (Example: *The lawyer said, "I'm the smartest man in the world..."*

Hand Surgery

Eleanor had majer surgry on both of her hands. When the docter came to check on her. She held up her heavilly bandeged hands and aksed, "Will I be able to play the piano when these bandeges come off"?

"I don't see why not," said the docter.

"How strange," said Eleanor. "I wasn't able to play the piano before!"

POSSIBLE CORRECTION:

Eleanor had major surgery on both of her hands. When the doctor came to check on her, she held up her heavily bandaged hands and asked, "Will I be able to play the piano when these bandages come off?"

"I don't see why not," said the doctor.

"How strange," said Eleanor. "I wasn't able to play the piano before!"

NOTES:
- This is a good exercise for practice correcting spelling errors.
- If a quotation is a question, the question mark goes inside the quotation marks.

The Optimist

Little katie was playing with her friend amber at ambers house. Katie through a ball in the living room and broke a lamp. She called her mother from ambers house to confess. But don't worry mom," said katie. "you don't have to worry about buying another one. Ambers mom said it was irreplaceable."

POSSIBLE CORRECTION:

Little Katie was playing with her friend Amber at Amber's house. Katie threw a ball in the living room and broke a lamp. She called her mother from Amber's house to confess. "But don't worry, Mom," said Katie. "You don't have to worry about buying another one. Amber's mom said it was irreplaceable."

NOTES:
- Nouns that show possession or ownership should have an apostrophe (*Amber's house*, for example).
- Quotation marks come in pairs. Use them at the beginning *and* at the end of the quotation.
- If a word in a line of dialogue is the first word of a sentence, it should be capitalized.

Three-Legged Chicken

A man driving home from work noticed that a chicken walking along the road had three legs. Following the chicken and ending up at a Farm. Getting out of his car and seeing that all the chickens on the Farm had three legs. He asked the farmer, "What's up with these chickens"? The farmer said, "Well everybody likes chicken legs, so I bread a three-legged bird. I'm going to be a millionaire." How do they taste asked the man. The farmer said, "I don't know. I haven't caught one yet.

POSSIBLE CORRECTION:

A man driving home from work noticed that a chicken walking along the road had three legs. He followed the chicken and ended up at a farm. Getting out of his car and seeing that all the chickens on the farm had three legs, he asked the farmer, "What's up with these chickens?"

The farmer said, "Well, everybody likes chicken legs, so I bred a three-legged bird. I'm going to be a millionaire."

"How do they taste?" asked the man.

The farmer said, "I don't know. I haven't caught one yet."

NOTES:
- Quotation marks come in pairs. Use them at the beginning *and* at the end of the quotation.
- Introductory words like *yes, no, oh, well,* etc. should be followed by a comma.
- When writing dialogue, start a new paragraph with each change of speakers.
- If a quotation is a question, the question mark goes inside the quotation marks.

Huffy Snail

A woman herd a knock at her front door. She opened the door and looked around but didn't see anyone. Then looked down and saw a snail. She picked it up and through it into the street.

Ten years later, the woman herd a knock at her door. She opened the door, and their sat the same snail. "What the heck was that all about," huffed the snail.

POSSIBLE CORRECTION:

A woman heard a knock at her front door. She opened the door and looked around but didn't see anyone. Then she looked down and saw a snail. She picked it up and threw it into the street.

Ten years later, the woman heard a knock at her door. She opened the door, and there sat the same snail. "What the heck was that all about?" huffed the snail.

NOTES:
- This paragraph contains spelling errors that a computer spell check would never catch.
- Normally, a comma would precede the words *huffed the snail*. However, since the quotation is a question, a question mark is used instead. A comma is not used with a question mark.

Frog Loan

A frog hopped into a bank and went too the teller window.

"How can I help you?" asked the teller, who's name was Patty Black.

"I would like a loan, to fix up my pad," said the frog.

"Do you have any collateral?" asked Patty Black.

"Sure," said the frog, holding up a small trinket.

Patty looked at the trinket and said, "I don't know. I'll have too clear this with the bank President."

When the President looked at the trinket, he said, "It's a knick-knack, Patty Black, give the frog a loan."

POSSIBLE CORRECTION:

A frog hopped into a bank and went to the teller window.

"How can I help you?" asked the teller, whose name was Patty Black.

"I would like a loan, to fix up my pad," said the frog.

"Do you have any collateral?" asked Patty Black.

"Sure," said the frog, holding up a small trinket.

Patty looked at the trinket and said, "I don't know. I'll have to clear this with the bank president."

When the president looked at the trinket, he said, "It's a knick-knack, Patty Black. Give the frog a loan."

NOTES:

- The story uses *too* when *to* is required. (A hint: *To*—with one *o*—is usually pronounced "tuh." When puzzling over which form to use, try plugging in *tuh*. If it sounds okay, *to* is probably the correct choice.)
- Titles like *president, captain, professor*, etc., are not capitalized unless used with the person's name (*Captain Elway* and *the captain*).

Manners

Cause she was running a bit late, mrs. snow asked her daughter abbie to answer the door and entertain too guests until she was ready. abbie invited the too woman into the living room and set down in front of them. she was about five years old and had a large nose freckles crooked teeth enormous glasses and very little hair on her head. She stared at the woman in silence.

The woman looked at her doubtfully. Finally, one of them muttered to the other, "she's not very P-R-E-T-T-Y, I fear," she said, carefully spelling the key word.

The little girl piped up, "But she's awfully S-M-A-R-T!"

POSSIBLE CORRECTION:

Because she was running a bit late, Mrs. Snow asked her daughter Abbie to answer the door and entertain two guests until she was ready. Abbie invited the two women into the living room and sat down in front of them. She was about five years old and had a large nose, freckles, crooked teeth, enormous glasses, and very little hair on her head. She stared at the women in silence.

The women looked at her doubtfully. Finally, one of them muttered to the other, "She's not very P-R-E-T-T-Y, I fear," she said, carefully spelling the key word.

The little girl piped up, "But she's awfully S-M-A-R-T!"

NOTES:
- *Cause* should be spelled *because.*
- Items in a series should be separated with commas.
- Proper nouns should begin with a capital letter.
- A person *sets* a table or *sets* something down. If referring to a person in a seated position, the word to use is *sits* or *sat.*

Pretzels

A women sold pretzels on a street corner four 25 since each. Every day a young man wood pass her pretzel stand and leave her a quarter. However he wood never take a pretzel.

This went on four more than five years, yet the too of them never spoke. One day as the man past the woman's pretzel stand, he left his quarter as usual. This time the pretzel woman spoke too him.

The woman, she said, "Sir, I appreciate you're business. You are a good customer, but I have too tell you that the pretzel price has increased to 35 since."

POSSIBLE CORRECTION:

A woman sold pretzels on a street corner for 25 cents each. Every day a young man would pass her pretzel stand and leave her a quarter. However, he would never take a pretzel.

This went on for more than five years, yet the two of them never spoke. One day as the man passed the woman's pretzel stand, he left his quarter as usual. This time the pretzel woman spoke to him.

The woman said, "Sir, I appreciate your business. You are a good customer, but I have to tell you that the pretzel price has increased to 35 cents."

NOTES:
- A computer spell check won't catch the spelling errors in this story.
- Avoid double subjects like "The woman, she."
- Use a comma after introductory words like *yes, no, however,* etc.

Animal Crackers

Little Robert and his Mother returned from the grocery store. They was putting away the groceries. Robert opened the box of animal crackers but spread them all over the table. Instead of eating them.

"What are you doing?" his Mother asked.

"The box says not to eat them if the seal is broken, the boy explained. "I'm looking for the seal.

POSSIBLE CORRECTION:

Little Robert and his mother returned from the grocery store. They were putting away the groceries. Robert opened the box of animal crackers but spread them all over the table instead of eating them.

"What are you doing?" his mother asked.

"The box says not to eat them if the seal is broken," the boy explained. "I'm looking for the seal."

NOTES:

- Capitalize *mother, father, grandmother, grandfather,* etc., only if they are used instead of the person's name (Yes: *He saw Mother.* No: *He saw his mother*).
- Many sentence fragments are formed simply because the writer puts a period in too soon. (Example: *Robert opened the box of animal crackers but spread them all over the table. Instead of eating them.*)
- Quotation marks come in pairs. Use them at the beginning *and* at the end of the quotation.

Chainsaw

A guy named Joe wanted to cut down some trees in his back yard. He went to a chainsaw shop and asked about the different chainsaws he saw displayed. The dealer said, "I have alot of different chainsaws, but you can save yourself alot of time and aggravation if you just go ahead and get this top-of-the-line model." "This chainsaw will cut a hundred cords of would for you in one day."

Thinking that sounded like good advice Joe bought the chainsaw. He took it home and began working on the trees. After working all day he had cut only too cords of wood. He was puzzled but decided to get up earlier the next day and try again.

The next day he got up at 4:00 a.m. and cut and cut until nightfall. However he managed to cut only three cords. He decided he must have a bad chainsaw.

The next day he took the chainsaw back to the dealer and complained. The dealer was baffled. "Only five cords of wood?" "I just don't understand it," he said. He took the chainsaw out of the case and looked it over. "It looks fine," he said. Then he started it up.

"What's that noise?" asked Joe.

Phunny Stuph • Copyright © 2005 Cottonwood Press, Inc. • 800-864-4297 • www.cottonwoodpress.com

48

Possible Correction:

A guy named Joe wanted to cut down some trees in his back yard. He went to a chainsaw shop and asked about the different chainsaws he saw displayed. The dealer said, "I have a lot of different chainsaws, but you can save yourself a lot of time and aggravation if you just go ahead and get this top-of-the-line model. This chainsaw will cut a hundred cords of wood for you in one day."

Thinking that sounded like good advice, Joe bought the chainsaw. He took it home and began working on the trees. After working all day, he had cut only two cords of wood. He was puzzled but decided to get up earlier the next day and try again.

The next day, he got up at 4:00 a.m. and cut and cut until nightfall. However, he managed to cut only three cords. He decided he must have a bad chainsaw.

The next day he took the chainsaw back to the dealer and complained. The dealer was baffled. "Only five cords of wood? I just don't understand it," he said. He took the chainsaw out of the case and looked it over. "It looks fine," he said. Then he started it up.

"What's that noise?" asked Joe.

Notes:

- The first set of quotation marks goes at the beginning of a line of dialogue. As long as the same person is speaking, no other quotation marks are needed until the end of the quotation, or until the quotation is interrupted with "he said" or other words to attribute the quote. In other words, you don't put quotation marks around every sentence.
- Introductory elements in a sentence should be followed by a comma. (Introductory elements include clauses, phrases, and introductory words like *yes, no, oh*, etc.)
- *A lot* is two words, not one.

Watching Out for Bears

The wyoming state department of fish and wildlife is advising hikers, hunters, fishermen, golfers, ect., to take extra precautions against bears when they are in the mountians near the towns of jackson cody and sheridan. "Wear noise-producing devices like little bells on your clothing," said a department representative at a recent talk. "You want to alert the bears to your presence but not startle them unexpectedly."

The representative went on to suggest that travelors carry pepper spray in case of an encounter with a bear. "Its also a good idea to watch for signs of bear activity," he said. Learn to recognize the difference between black bear and grizzly bear droppings."

"How do you tell the diffrence?" asked one audience member.

"Thats easy," said the ramger. "black bear droppings are smaller and contain berries and possibly squirrel fur. Grizzly bear droppings have bells in them and smell like pepper spray.

POSSIBLE CORRECTION:

The Wyoming State Department of Fish and Wildlife is advising hikers, hunters, fishermen, golfers, etc., to take extra precautions against bears when they are in the mountains near the towns of Jackson, Cody, and Sheridan. "Wear noise-producing devices like little bells on your clothing," said a department representative at a recent talk. "You want to alert the bears to your presence but not startle them unexpectedly."

The representative went on to suggest that travelers carry pepper spray in case of an encounter with a bear. "It's also a good idea to watch for signs of bear activity," he said. "Learn to recognize the difference between black bear and grizzly bear droppings."

"How do you tell the difference?" asked one audience member.

"That's easy," said the ranger. "Black bear droppings are smaller and contain berries and possibly squirrel fur. Grizzly bear droppings have bells in them and smell like pepper spray."

NOTES:
- Capitalize titles of departments, buildings, organizations, etc.
- *Etc.* is the correct spelling for what many people think is *ect.* It is followed by a comma if used in the middle of a sentence.
- *It's* is the proper spelling when *it is* can be substituted in the sentence. *That's* is the correct spelling when *that is* can be substituted.
- Capitalize the first word in a sentence included in a line of dialogue.
- Items in a series should be separated with commas.

Biscuit Bomb

an urban legend

A lady named Linda. Visiting her in-laws and went into a local supermarket to pick up some groceries. Hot day, but later noticed by several people sitting in car with windows rolled up and eyes closed. With both hands behind back of her head. Another customer becoming concerned. Then noticing Linda's eyes now open. Looking strange. Asking her if she was okay.

Replied, "Shot in back of head. Holding my brains in for over an hour."

Man reaching paramedics. No help because car doors locked and Linda refusing to remove hands. Finally getting into car. Discover wad of bread dough on back of head. Empty Pillsbury biscuit canister in back seat. Exploded in heat. Hit her in back of head. Sounded like gunshot. Thought she had been hit, reached for head. Felt bread dough, and tried to hold on to brains. Passed out. Later woke up, still trying to hold on to brains.

POSSIBLE CORRECTION:

A lady named Linda was visiting her in-laws and went into a local supermarket to pick up some groceries. Several people later noticed her sitting in the car with her eyes closed and the windows rolled up, even though it was a hot day. She also had both hands behind the back of her head. One of the customers became concerned when he saw Linda again and noticed that her eyes were now open. She was looking strange, so he tapped on the window and asked her if she was okay.

She replied, "I was shot in the back of the head. I've been holding my brains in for over an hour."

The man reached paramedics, who were no help at first because the car doors were locked and Linda refused to remove her hands. When they finally got into the car, they discovered a wad of bread dough on the back of her head and an empty Pillsbury biscuit canister in the back seat. It had exploded in the heat and hit her in the back of the head. She thought the sound was a gunshot and that she had been hit. She reached for her head and felt bread dough. She then held on with both hands, trying to hold on to her brains. She passed out. Later, she woke up, still holding on and trying to keep her brains from falling out.

NOTES:

This exercise is an excellent one for practice correcting sentence fragments. Every "sentence" in the original is a fragment.

Dad and the Diaper

A man and a woman were the proud parents of a newborn son. One saturday the mother had to go out to do some errands, so the proud father stayed home to watch his new son. He was kinda nervous, but his wife insisted he would do just fine.

Soon after the mother left the baby started to cry. The father did everything he could think of, but the baby just wouldn't stop crying. He tried to call his wife on her cell phone, but she didn't answer. Finally the dad got so worried he decided to take the infant to the emergency room.

After the Doctor listened to all the father had done to get the baby to stop crying he began to examine the babys ears, chest, and nose. Finally he went down to the diaper area. When he opened the diaper he found it was quite full.

"Here's the problem," the Doctor explained. "He just needs to be changed."

The perplexed father said, "But the diaper package specifically says it's good for up to 10 pounds!"

Possible Correction:

A man and a woman were the proud parents of a newborn son. One Saturday, the mother had to go out to do some errands, so the proud father stayed home to watch his new son. He was kind of nervous, but his wife insisted he would do just fine.

Soon after the mother left, the baby started to cry. The father did everything he could think of, but the baby just wouldn't stop crying. He tried to call his wife on her cell phone, but she didn't answer. Finally, the dad got so worried he decided to take the infant to the emergency room.

After the doctor listened to all the father had done to get the baby to stop crying, he began to examine the baby's ears, chest, and nose. Finally, he went down to the diaper area. When he opened the diaper, he found it was quite full.

"Here's the problem," the doctor explained. "He just needs to be changed."

The perplexed father said, "But the diaper package specifically says it's good for up to 10 pounds!"

Notes:

- *Kind of* should replace *kinda.*
- *Doctor* is capitalized only when it is used with the doctor's name, as in *Doctor Evans.*
- Introductory elements in a sentence should be followed by a comma. (Introductory elements include clauses, phrases, and introductory words like *yes, no, oh,* etc.)
- Use an apostrophe to indicate possession or ownership (*baby's ears, chest and nose*).

Hard Workers

A man traveling across the country stopped a rest stop and took a brake. As he stood by his car drinking a pepsi, he watched a couple of men working along the roadside. One man would dig a hole two or three feet deep. Then the other man would come along behind him and fill the hole. While one was digging a new hole, the other was always about 25 feet behind filling in the old. The traveler finished his pepsi and headed down the road toward the men. "Can you tell me what's going on here with this digging?" he asked. "We work for the county," one of the men answered. But one of you is digging a hole, and the other is filling it up. Your not accomplishing anything. Aren't you wasting the county's money?" "You don't understand," one of the men said, leaning on his shovel and wiping the sweet off his brow. "Normally there's three of us—Henry, Clayton, and me. I dig the hole. Henry sticks in the tree, and Clayton here puts the dirt back." "The traveler looked puzzled.The man continued. "Just because Henry's sick doesn't mean we shouldn't work now!"

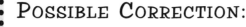

Possible Correction:

A man traveling across the country stopped at a rest stop and took a break. As he stood by his car drinking a Pepsi, he watched a couple of men working along the roadside. One man would dig a hole two or three feet deep. Then the other man would come along behind him and fill the hole. While one was digging a new hole, the other was always about 25 feet behind filling in the old.

The traveler finished his Pepsi and headed down the road toward the men. "Can you tell me what's going on here with this digging?" he asked.

"We work for the county," one of the men answered.

"But one of you is digging a hole, and the other is filling it up. You're not accomplishing anything. Aren't you wasting the county's money?"

"You don't understand," one of the men said, leaning on his shovel and wiping the sweat off his brow. "Normally, there's three of us—Henry, Clayton, and me. I dig the hole. Henry sticks in the tree, and Clayton here puts the dirt back."

The traveler looked puzzled.

The man continued. "Just because Henry's sick doesn't mean we shouldn't work now!"

Notes:
- Brand names of products should be capitalized.
- When writing dialogue, start a new paragraph with each change of speakers.
- *You're* is a contraction of *you are*. Use *you're* when *you are* can be substituted in a sentence.

Telling the Truth

A large family with eight children moved to a new city, they had a difficult time finding an apartment. Many apartments were large enough but the landlords always objected too such a large family.

After several days of searching the father asked the mother to take the five younger children to visit the cemetery, he took the older three to find an apartment.

After they had looked most of the morning the father found a place that was just right. Then the landlord asked the usual question: "How many children do you have"

The father answered with a deep sigh, "Eight..."

"My goodness," the landlord interrupted. "I can't..."

The father continued, "...but five are with their deer mother in the cemetary."

He got the apartment.

Possible Correction:

A large family with eight children moved to a new city. They had a difficult time finding an apartment. Many apartments were large enough, but the landlords always objected to such a large family.

After several days of searching, the father asked the mother to take the five younger children to visit the cemetery while he took the older three to find an apartment.

After they had looked most of the morning, the father found a place that was just right. Then the landlord asked the usual question: "How many children do you have?"

The father answered with a deep sigh, "Eight..."

"My goodness," the landlord interrupted. "I can't..."

The father continued, "...but five are with their dear mother in the cemetery."

He got the apartment.

Notes:

- A *deer* is an animal. Therefore, the father should be referring to the children's *dear mother*.
- A comma should not be used to separate two sentences. Use a period, a semicolon, or a comma with *and, but, or, for* or *nor*.
- Use a comma before the conjunction in a compound sentence. A compound sentence is two complete sentences connected with *and, but, or, for,* or *nor.* (Example: *Many apartments were large enough, but the landlords always objected to such a large family.*)

Tranquilized Cat

an urban legend

A woman going on a plane trip and taking her cat in a carrier. Worried about how the cat would act. She mentioned her worry to her doctor at her appointment and he thought a minute and then took out a tranquilizer pill and broke it in half and told her to give the half to the cat before take-off and told her it would probably calm the cat right down. Later the doctor talking to his friend who was a veterinarian. The vet said, "You didn't really do that, did you? That kind of tranquilizer has the opposite effect on a cat. The cat will be a clawing mess!" The next time the woman saw her doctor. Told the doctor she had given the cat the tranquilizer. Said, "He was so wild on the plane that we thought he was going to jump out of his skin. It was all I could do to keep him in the carrier, and he yowled the whole trip." The doctor was about to apologize but before he could get any words out the woman continued and thanked him profusely and he was puzzled by that since the cat had been so wild but then the woman said, "I am so grateful for that pill. I can't imagine how the cat would have behaved without it!" Doctor sighing in relief.

POSSIBLE CORRECTION:

A woman was going on a plane trip and taking her cat in a carrier. She was worried about how the cat would act, so she mentioned her worry to her doctor at her appointment. He thought a minute and then took out a tranquilizer pill. He broke it in half and told her to give the half to the cat before take-off. He told her it would probably calm the cat right down.

Later, the doctor was talking to his friend, who was a veterinarian. The veterinarian said, "You didn't really do that, did you? That kind of tranquilizer has the opposite effect on a cat. The cat will be a clawing mess!"

The next time the woman saw her doctor, she told him she had given the cat the tranquilizer. She said, "He was so wild on the plane that we thought he was going to jump out of his skin. It was all I could do to keep him in the carrier, and he yowled the whole trip." The doctor was about to apologize, but before he could get any words out, the woman continued, thanking him profusely. The doctor was puzzled, since she said the cat had been so wild. Then the woman said, "I'm so grateful for that pill. I can't imagine how the cat would have behaved without it!"

The doctor sighed with relief.

NOTES:

This exercise is an excellent one for practice in correcting run-ons and fragments.

On the Run from a Bear

Two campers are walking through the woods when a huge brown bear suddenly appeared about 50 feet in front of them.

The bear sees the campers and began to head toward them.

The first camper drops her backpack, digs out a pair of sneakers, and frantically began to put them on. The second camper says, "What are you doing? Sneakers won't help you outrun that bear."

"I don't need to outrun the bear," the first camper said. "I just need to outrun *you*."

POSSIBLE CORRECTION:

Two campers are walking through the woods when a huge brown bear suddenly appears about 50 feet in front of them.

The bear sees the campers and begins to head toward them.

The first camper drops her backpack, digs out a pair of sneakers, and frantically begins to put them on. The second camper says, "What are you doing? Sneakers won't help you outrun that bear."

"I don't need to outrun the bear," the first camper says. "I just need to outrun *you*."

NOTES:

This is a good exercise for correcting errors in tense. Students should rewrite the piece so that it is all in present tense or all in past tense. (Present tense verbs can be substituted in this sentence: Today I _____. Past tense verbs can be substituted in this sentence: Yesterday I _____. Future tense verbs can be substituted in this sentence: Tomorrow I _____.)

Grounding

An irritated father complained to his friend that kids today have it to easy. "When I was a kid," he said, "My parents sent me to my room without supper if I misbehaved. But my son has his own color TV a telephone a computer and a CD player in his room!"

"How do you handle it"? his friend asked.

"I send him to *my* room!"

POSSIBLE CORRECTION:

An irritated father complained to his friend that kids today have it too easy. "When I was a kid," he said, "my parents sent me to my room without supper if I misbehaved. But my son has his own color TV, a telephone, a computer, and a CD player in his room!"

"How do you handle it?" his friend asked.

"I send him to *my* room!"

NOTES:

- Capitalize the first word of a line of dialogue only when it begins a sentence. In the first paragraph above, *my parents sent me to my room without supper* is a continuation of the sentence that begins *When I was a kid*.
- Items in a series should be separated with commas.
- If a quotation is a question, put a question mark inside the quotation marks.

A Great Excuse

This past Fall semester at duke university, two Sophomores were doing very well in their Chemistry class. Although the final exam was on Monday, they decided to go up to the university of virginia that weekend to see some friends.

The Sophomores had a great time, but they overslept and didn't make it back in time for the final exam. When they returned in the Afternoon, they found Professor Aldrich and told him they'd had a flat tire on the way back. "We would of been here on time, but we didn't have a spare and couldn't get help for a long time."

The Professor thought this over and then agreed that they could make up the final on the following day. The two students were elated and relieved.

The next day the Professor placed them in seperate rooms and handed each of them a test booklet. "You may begin," he said.

They looked at the first problem, which was worth five points. Each answered it easy. "Cool!" they thought." "this is going to be easy." Each of them completed the problem and turned the page.

They weren't prepared for the only remaining question, worth 95 points. It said, "Which tire?"

POSSIBLE CORRECTION:

This past fall semester at Duke University, two sophomores were doing very well in their chemistry class. Although the final exam was on Monday, they decided to go up to the University of Virginia that weekend to see some friends.

The sophomores had a great time, but they overslept and didn't make it back in time for the final exam. When they returned in the afternoon, they found Professor Aldrich and told him they'd had a flat tire on the way back. "We would have been here on time, but we didn't have a spare and couldn't get help for a long time."

The professor thought this over and then agreed that they could make up the final on the following day. The two students were elated and relieved.

The next day the professor placed them in separate rooms and handed each of them a test booklet. "You may begin," he said.

They looked at the first problem, which was worth five points. Each answered it easily. "Cool!" they thought. "This is going to be easy." Each of them completed the problem and turned the page.

They weren't prepared for the only remaining question, worth 95 points. It said, "Which tire?"

NOTES:

- School subjects are not capitalized unless they are (a) also the name of a language or (b) the title of a certain class. (Examples: *English, Introduction to Algebra II, geometry, science, Advanced Auto Mechanics 201, art*.)
- Names of institutions like universities should be capitalized.
- *Relieved* follows the "i" before "e" except after "c" rule.
- *Separate* is a very commonly misspelled word. Correctly spelled, there is *a rat* in the word (*sep**arat**e*).
- *Easily*, not *easy*, is the word to use to describe how something was done. (*Easily* is an adverb. Adverbs describe verbs. *Easy* is an adjective.)
- Months of the year are capitalized, but seasons are not.

The Imposter

a famous scientist from alamagordo new mexico was on his way to a seminar to give another lecture on his new breakthrough in research. His chaueffer saw how tired he looked and felt sorry for him. "Sir why don't you take the day off today"? he sugested. "I've herd you're lecture so many times by now that I no it by heart. I can give the lecture, and you can just sit back and relax."

Because the scientist was very tired of giving the same lecture over and over again. He thought this was a great idea.

The scientist put on the chaueffer's hat and sat down in the back of the lecture hall. The chaueffer went to the podium, he gave a excellent lecture. Imitating the scientist. He asked for questions at the end.

A professor in the hall stood up and asked a long, complicated, technical question. The chaueffer at first panicked inside, but he managed to pull himself together. "That is a very simple question," he replied. "It is so simple even my chaueffer can answer it. Sir?"

POSSIBLE CORRECTION:

A famous scientist from Alamogordo, New Mexico, was on his way to a seminar to give another lecture on his new breakthrough in research. His chauffeur saw how tired he looked and felt sorry for him. "Sir, why don't you take the day off today?" he suggested. "I've heard your lecture so many times by now that I know it by heart. I can give the lecture, and you can just sit back and relax."

Because the scientist was very tired of giving the same lecture over and over again, he thought this was a great idea.

The scientist put on the chauffeur's hat and sat down in the back of the lecture hall. The chauffeur went to the podium and gave an excellent lecture, imitating the scientist. He asked for questions at the end.

A professor in the hall stood up and asked a long, complicated, technical question. The chauffeur at first panicked inside, but he managed to pull himself together. "That is a very simple question," he replied. "It is so simple even my chauffeur can answer it. Sir?"

NOTES:
This exercise includes a wide variety of errors: sentence fragments, run-on sentences, spelling, usage, etc.

Zookeeper

A zookeeper approached three boys standing near the lions cage. He was afraid they were up to no good, so he asked them to tell him their names and what they were doing. The first boy said, my name's Ryan, and I was trying to feed peanuts to the lions. The second boy said, my name's Jake, and I was trying to feed peanuts to the lions. The third boy said, my name is Peanuts.

POSSIBLE CORRECTION:

A zookeeper approached three boys standing near the lions' cage. He was afraid they were up to no good, so he asked them to tell him their names and what they were doing. The first boy said, "My name's Ryan, and I was trying to feed peanuts to the lions."

The second boy said, "My name's Jake, and I was trying to feed peanuts to the lions."

The third boy said, "My name is Peanuts."

NOTES:
- Use an apostrophe to indicate possession or ownership, as in *lions' cage*. (Note that the apostrophe comes *after* the s here because the cage belongs to more than one lion. *Lion's cage* would mean the cage belonged to only one lion.)
- When writing dialogue, start a new paragraph with each change of speakers.

What Are Dogs Good For?

A nursry skool teecher wuz standin on the playgrownd won dae wen a fire truk zumed passed. A Dalmashun dog sat in the frunt seet. The childrun started taking about the Dogs Duties.

"They use him to keep crouds back," said one Child.

"No," said unother Child. "he's just for good luck."

A third Child brot the arguement to a cloze. "They use the Dog," she said firmly, "to find the fire hidrant."

> ## POSSIBLE CORRECTION:
>
> A nursery school teacher was standing on the playground one day when a fire truck zoomed past. A Dalmatian dog sat in the front seat. The children started talking about the dog's duties.
>
> "They use him to keep crowds back," said one child.
>
> "No," said another child. "He's just for good luck."
>
> A third child brought the argument to a close. "They use the dog," she said firmly, "to find the fire hydrant."

NOTES:

The exercise is a good one to show how numerous misspelled words and incorrect capitalization can make something difficult to read.

Investment in the Future

A motorist driving by a ranch hit and killed a calf that was crossing the rode. The driver, went to the owner of the calf, and explayned what had happened. He then asked what the animal was worth "Oh, about $200 today," said the rancher. "In six years, though, it would of been worth $900. So $900 is what I'm out." The motorist sat down, and wrote out a check. and handed it to the farmer. "Here," he said, "is the check for $900, it's postdated, six years from now."

POSSIBLE CORRECTION:

A motorist, driving by a ranch, hit and killed a calf that was crossing the road. The driver went to the owner of the calf and explained what had happened. He then asked what the animal was worth. "Oh, about $200 today," said the rancher. "In six years, though, it would have been worth $900. So $900 is what I'm out."

The motorist sat down and wrote out a check and handed it to the farmer. "Here," he said, "is the check for $900. It's postdated six years from now."

NOTES:
- This exercise has many unnecessary commas.
- *Would of* should be written *would've* or *would have.*

Coffee Break

A mother was surprized when her seven-year-old old son made her cofee one Winter morning. She drank what was the worst kup of coffee in her life. When she got to the bottom she saw three little green plastic armie men. She asked him why they were in her coffee cup.

The little boy said, "They say on television that "The best part of waking up is Soldiers in your cup.""

....

POSSIBLE CORRECTION:

A mother was surprised when her seven-year-old son made her coffee one winter morning. She drank what was the worst cup of coffee in her life. When she got to the bottom, she saw three little green plastic army men. She asked him why they were in her coffee cup.

The little boy said, "They say on television that 'The best part of waking up is soldiers in your cup.'"

....

NOTES:
- Months of the year are capitalized. Seasons are not.
- When a quotation includes *another* quotation, the second quotation has single quotation marks around it.

Plane Trip

sarah had spent a week visiting her Father and Stepmother in denver. Her Father and her seven-year-old nephew went with her when she returned to denver international airport for the flight home. After checking in at the counter Sarah walked back to her relatives to tell them she was going to hafta wait an additional three hours in the airport.

"How come?" asked her nephew.

"My plane has been grounded," explained Sarah.

"Grounded?" said her nephew. "I didn't know planes had parents.

POSSIBLE CORRECTION:

Sarah had spent a week visiting her father and stepmother in Denver. Her father and her seven-year-old nephew went with her when she returned to Denver International Airport for the flight home. After checking in at the counter, Sarah walked back to her relatives to tell them she was going to have to wait an additional three hours in the airport.

"How come?" asked her nephew.

"My plane has been grounded," explained Sarah.

"Grounded?" said her nephew. "I didn't know planes had parents."

NOTES:
- Capitalize the names of cities.
- Capitalize the names of specific places. (No: *the airport.* Yes: *Denver International Airport*)
- Capitalize *mother, father, grandmother, grandfather* only if they are used instead of the person's name (Yes: *He saw Mother.* No: *He saw his mother*).
- *Hafta* should be written *have to.*

Babies

a gril in the frist grade came home from school & told her mother that she had a new teacher.

"thats nice" said her mother. "did you learn anything knew"?

"yes," said the little girl. "she tought us how to make babies."

The mother was shoked. Very cautoiusly she asked, "how do you make babies then?

Its easy," said the girl. "You just take off the 'y' and add 'ies.'"

> ## POSSIBLE CORRECTION:
>
> A girl in the first grade came home from school and told her mother that she had a new teacher.
>
> "That's nice," said her mother. "Did you learn anything new?"
>
> "Yes," said the little girl. "She taught us how to make babies."
>
> The mother was shocked. Very cautiously she asked, "How do you make babies then?"
>
> "It's easy," said the girl. "You just take off the 'y' and add 'ies.'"

NOTES:
- *That's* and *it's* each need an apostrophe here, since they are substituting for *that is* and *it is*.
- A number of spelling errors need to be corrected.
- If a quotation is a question, the question mark goes inside the quotation marks.
- Don't use symbols like "&" in formal writing. Spell out *and*.

The Magician and the Parrot

A magician working on a cruise ship in the Caribbean had a different audience each week. That made his job easy. He just did the same tricks over and over again.

The problem was the captain's parrot. The parrot saw the same shows each week and began to figure out how the magician did each trick. As soon as he figured out a trick, he would shout out his discovery in the middle of the show. One night he shouted, "Look! It's not the same hat!" Another night he shouted, "He's hiding the flowers under the chair!" Another night he announced, "Every single card in the deck is the queen of hearts!"

The magician was furious. He hated the parrot more and more, but he couldn't do anything about it because the parrot was the captain's parrot.

Then the ship was in a freak accident and sank. The magician wound up sitting on a piece of wood in the middle of the ocean—with the parrot. They stared at each other with hate, but neither of them said a word. This went on day after day.

Finally, after a week, the parrot said, "Okay, I give up. Where's the boat?"

POSSIBLE CORRECTION:

A magician working on a cruise ship in the Caribbean had a different audience each week. That made his job easy. He just did the same tricks over and over again.

The problem was the captain's parrot. The parrot saw the same shows each week and began to figure out how the magician did each trick. As soon as he figured out a trick, he would shout out his discovery in the middle of the show. One night he shouted, "Look! It's not the same hat!" Another night he shouted, "He's hiding the flowers under the chair!" Another night he announced, "Every single card in the deck is the queen of hearts!"

The magician was furious. He hated the parrot more and more, but he couldn't do anything about it because the parrot was the captain's parrot.

Then the ship was in a freak accident and sank. The magician wound up sitting on a piece of wood in the middle of the ocean— with the parrot. They stared at each other with hate, but neither of them said a word. This went on day after day.

Finally, after a week, the parrot said, "Okay, I give up. Where's the boat?"

NOTES:

Use this only if you really want to challenge your students. There are *no* errors in this piece!

Skydiver

A man goes skydiving for the first time. He jumped out of the plane, counts to ten, pulls the ripcord, & nothing happened. Not to worried yet. He pulls the cord for the auxiliary parashute. However that chute doesn't appear, either. As the man is plummeting toward the ground, he is amazed to see a woman coming up the other way.

"Do you know anything about parachutes" he shouts to her.

"no," she answers. "do you know anything about gas stoves"

POSSIBLE CORRECTION:

A man went skydiving for the first time. He jumped out of the plane, counted to ten, pulled the ripcord, and nothing happened. He wasn't worried yet. He pulled the cord for the auxiliary parachute. However, that chute didn't appear, either. As the man was plummeting toward the ground, he was amazed to see a woman coming up the other way.

"Do you know anything about parachutes?" he shouted to her.

"No," she answered. "Do you know anything about gas stoves?"

NOTES:
* This is a good exercise for practice in sticking to one tense. The piece should be rewritten so that it is entirely in present tense or entirely in past tense.
* Use a question mark after a quotation that asks a question.
* Use a comma after introductory words like *yes, no, oh, however, well, nevertheless,* etc. (Example: *However, that chute didn't appear, either.*)

The Parking Ticket

I went to the store the other day and I was only in there for about five minutes but when I came out there was a motorcycle cop writing a parking ticket so I went up to him and said, "How about giving a guy a break?" but he ignored me and continued writing the ticket, so I called him a stupid idiot and he glared at me and started writing another ticket for having bald tires! Then I really got angry at him and told him he was a jerk and he started writing a third ticket, and this went on for about 20 minutes and the more names I called him, the more tickets he wrote, but I didn't care because *my* car was parked around the corner.

POSSIBLE CORRECTION:

I went to the store the other day. I was only in there for about five minutes, but when I came out, there was a motorcycle cop writing a parking ticket. I went up to him and said, "How about giving a guy a break?" He ignored me and continued writing the ticket, so I called him a stupid idiot. He glared at me and started writing another ticket for having bald tires. Then I really got angry at him and told him he was a jerk. He started writing a third ticket!

This went on for about 20 minutes, and the more names I called him, the more tickets he wrote. I didn't care, though, because *my* car was parked around the corner.

NOTES:
This exercise gives students practice in correcting run-on sentences.

Respect

· ·

a teacher injured his back one summer, and had to wear a plaster cast around the upper part of his body. Because he wore it under his shirt it was not noticeable at all.

On the frist day of school he found himself assigned to what was supposebly the toughest class in the whole district. Walking confidently into the rowdy classroom he opened the window as wide as possible and then looked down at his class list. The students started talking and joking around, and he told them to settle down They became louder. He told them again to settle down. They became even louder. He told them again to settle down. This time they just laughed at him.

While all this was going on a strong breeze from the window was making his tie flap annoyingly. He kept grabbing it and rearranging it, but it still flaped. Finally he stood up took a big stapler off his desk and stapled the tie to his chest in several places.

Discipline was not a problem from that moment on.

· ·

POSSIBLE CORRECTION:

A teacher injured his back one summer and had to wear a plaster cast around the upper part of his body. Because he wore it under his shirt, it was not noticeable at all.

On the first day of school, he found himself assigned to what was supposedly the toughest class in the whole district. Walking confidently into the rowdy classroom, he opened the window as wide as possible and then looked down at his class list. The students started talking and joking around, and he told them to settle down. They became louder. He told them again to settle down. They became even louder. He told them again to settle down. This time, they just laughed at him.

While all this was going on, a strong breeze from the window was making his tie flap annoyingly. He kept grabbing it and rearranging it, but it still flapped. Finally, he stood up, took a big stapler off his desk, and stapled the tie to his chest in several places.

Discipline was not a problem from that moment on.

NOTES:

- Introductory elements like phrases and clauses should be followed by a comma. (Example: *Because he wore it under his shirt, it was not noticeable at all.*)
- A common error made in both speech and writing is to put a "b" in the word *supposedly*.
- For one-syllable words ending in a consonant preceded by a vowel, the consonant is generally doubled when adding "ed" or "ing" (*flapped, flapping*).

Elephant Joke

A little girl asked a scientist, "How do you catch a white elephant?"

"Go to a place where there are white elephants," said the scientist. "Bring along a muffin, with raisins. Climb a tree. When the white elephant is close, drop the muffin in front of it. It will be happy and eat the muffin. White elephants like muffins with raisins. Repeat this procedure for five days in a row."

"After the fifth day, the white elephant will be use to receiving its daily muffin with raisins. On the sixth day, climb the tree. This time bring along a muffin *without* raisins and drop it. When the white elephant finds out that the muffin lacks raisins, it will darken in anger."

"Then what?" asked the little girl.

"Then you catch it the same way you catch an ordinary gray elephant," he said.

POSSIBLE CORRECTION:

A little girl asked a scientist, "How do you catch a white elephant?"

"Go to a place where there are white elephants," said the scientist. "Bring along a muffin, with raisins. Climb a tree. When the white elephant is close, drop the muffin in front of it. It will be happy and eat the muffin. White elephants like muffins with raisins. Repeat this procedure for five days in a row."

"After the fifth day, the white elephant will be used to receiving its daily muffin with raisins. On the sixth day, climb the tree. This time bring along a muffin *without* raisins and drop it. When the white elephant finds out that the muffin lacks raisins, it will darken in anger."

"Then what?" asked the little girl.

"Then you catch it the same way you catch an ordinary gray elephant," he said.

NOTES:

There is only *one* error in this story: *use to* should be *used to.*

Advice from a Cow

A mans car stalled on a country road one morning. When he got out to fix it, a cow comes along & stopped beside him. "Your trouble is probably in the carburetor," said the cow. Startled, the man jumped back & ran down the road until he met a farmer. The amazed man tells the farmer his story. "Was it a large read cow with a brown spot over the right eye?" asked the farmer. "Yes, yes," the man replied. "Oh I wouldn't listen to Bessie," said the farmer. "She doesn't know a thing about cars."

POSSIBLE CORRECTION:

A man's car stalled on a country road one morning. When he got out to fix it, a cow came along and stopped beside him. "Your trouble is probably in the carburetor," said the cow. Startled, the man jumped back and ran down the road until he met a farmer. The amazed man told the farmer his story.

"Was it a large red cow with a brown spot over the right eye?" asked the farmer.

"Yes, yes," the man replied.

"Oh, I wouldn't listen to Bessie," said the farmer. "She doesn't know a thing about cars."

NOTES:

- Use an apostrophe with nouns that show ownership or possession (*a man's car*).
- Use the same tense throughout a story. The story should be corrected so that it is written entirely in present tense *or* in past tense.
- Use a comma after introductory words like *yes, no, oh, well*, etc.
- Don't use symbols like "&" in formal writing. Spell out *and*.

Thirsty Tourist

A tourist became seperated from his travel group in the middle of the sahara. He begged a passing nomad for water.

"Sorry," said the nomad. "I don't have any water, but I do have a selection of lovely ties for sale."

"Are you crazy?" cryed the tourist. Not believing the nomads cruelty. Soon he saw another nomad. "Water!" he gasped. Close to death from thirst. "Please give me some water."

"I have no water," the nomad replied. "However I do have these handsome ties I would be glad to sell to you."

The tourist shook his head in disbelief, and stumbled on. Soon he saw a magnificent Hotel far in the distance. He managed to crawl at last into the lobby and croaked, "Please give me water."

"I'm sorry, sir," said the doorman. "we don't let anyone in without a tie."

POSSIBLE CORRECTION:

A tourist became separated from his travel group in the middle of the Sahara. He begged a passing nomad for water.

"Sorry," said the nomad. "I don't have any water, but I do have a selection of lovely ties for sale."

"Are you crazy?" cried the tourist, not believing the nomad's cruelty. Soon he saw another nomad. "Water!" he gasped, close to death from thirst. "Please give me some water."

"I have no water," the nomad replied. "However, I do have these handsome ties I would be glad to sell to you."

The tourist shook his head in disbelief and stumbled on. Soon he saw a magnificent hotel far in the distance. He managed to crawl at last into the lobby and croaked, "Please give me water."

"I'm sorry, sir," said the doorman. "We don't let anyone in without a tie."

NOTES:
- When spelled correctly, there is *a rat* in *separate* or *separated* (sep**arat**ed).
- Many sentence fragments occur simply because the writer has separated a phrase or clause from the rest of a sentence. (Example: *"Are you crazy?" cryed the tourist. Not believing the nomads cruelty.* Corrected: *"Are you crazy?" cried the tourist, not believing the nomad's cruelty.*)
- There is no need for a comma in compound verbs. (*The tourist **shook** his head in disbelief and **stumbled** on.*)
- Capitalize the names of specific places (*Sahara*).
- Use a comma after introductory words like *yes, no, oh, well, however,* etc.

Impressing the Clients

A young businessman had just started his own firm. He'd rented a beautiful office & had it furnished with antiques! Sitting in his office one day, he saw a man come into the reception area. Wishing to appear busy the businessman picked up the phone & started to pretend he had a big deal working! He threw huge figures around & made giant commitments. Finally, he hangs up and asked the visitor, "Can I help you?" The man said, "Sure. I've come to install the phone."

POSSIBLE CORRECTION:

A young businessman had just started his own firm. He'd rented a beautiful office and had it furnished with antiques. Sitting in his office one day, he saw a man come into the reception area. Wishing to appear busy, the businessman picked up the phone and started to pretend he had a big deal working. He threw huge figures around and made giant commitments. Finally, he hung up and asked the visitor, "Can I help you?"

The man said, "Sure. I've come to install the phone."

NOTES:
- Exclamation points should be used sparingly. Only the last sentence in the above story might merit an exclamation point, and even that one isn't essential.
- The story starts out in past tense. Then, suddenly, it switches to present tense with *hangs*. The word should be the past tense, *hung*.
- Don't use symbols like "&" in formal writing. Spell out *and*.

Prison Jokes

It was a man's frist day in prison. Puzzled to hear other inmates roaring with laughter every time someone called out a number. He asked his cellmate what was happening.

"We no all our jokes so well becuz we have heard them all so often. To save time retelling them we have numbered them," he answered.

The newcomer thot he would join in. He shouted, "208!" He was amazed when everyone in the prison started shaking with laughter. The cellmate wiped tears from his eyes and said, "We hadn't heard that one before."

POSSIBLE CORRECTION:

It was a man's first day in prison. Puzzled to hear other inmates roaring with laughter every time someone called out a number, he asked his cellmate what was happening.

"We know all our jokes so well because we have heard them all so often. To save time retelling them, we have numbered them," he answered.

The newcomer thought he would join in. He shouted, "208!" He was amazed when everyone in the prison started shaking with laughter.

The cellmate wiped tears from his eyes and said, "We hadn't heard that one before."

NOTES:

- *First* is often misspelled as *frist* in student papers.
- Introductory elements like phrases and clauses should be followed by a comma. (*To save time retelling them, we have numbered them.*)
- Many sentences fragments occur simply because the writer has separated a phrase or clause from the rest of a sentence. (Example: *Puzzled to hear other inmates roaring with laughter every time someone called out a number. He asked his cellmate what was happening.* Corrected: *"Puzzled to hear other inmates roaring with laughter every time someone called out a number, he asked his cellmate what was happening.*)

The Art Collector

A art collector is walking through the city when he notices a mangy cat lapping milk from a sawser in the doorway of a store. He can't beleive his eyes. The saucer is very old & very valuable. Trying to stay calm he walks into the store & offers to buy the cat for two dollars.

The store owner replies, "I'am sorry, but the cat isn't for sale."

The art collector says, "I have a mouse problem in my house, & I really, really need a hungry cat. I'll pay you twenty dollars for that one."

"Sold," said the owner. And hands over the cat.

The collector continues, "Hey, for the twenty bucks I wonder if you could throw in that old sawser. The cat's used to it, & it'll save me having to get a dish."

"Sorry," said the owner, "but that's my lucky sawser. So far this week I've sold sixty-eight cats."

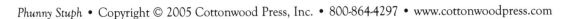

Phunny Stuph • Copyright © 2005 Cottonwood Press, Inc. • 800-864-4297 • www.cottonwoodpress.com
86

Possible Correction:

An art collector is walking through the city when he notices a mangy cat lapping milk from a saucer in the doorway of a store. He can't believe his eyes. The saucer is very old and very valuable. Trying to stay calm, he walks into the store and offers to buy the cat for two dollars.

The store owner replies, "I'm sorry, but the cat isn't for sale."

The art collector says, "I have a mouse problem in my house, and I really, really need a hungry cat. I'll pay you twenty dollars for that one."

"Sold," says the owner, and he hands over the cat.

The collector continues, "Hey, for the twenty bucks, I wonder if you could throw in that old saucer. The cat's used to it, and it'll save me having to get a dish."

"Sorry," said the owner, "but that's my lucky saucer. So far this week I've sold sixty-eight cats."

Notes:

- Use *an*, not *a*, before words starting with a vowel sound.
- *Believe* follows the "i" before "e" except after "c" rule.
- Write *I am* or *I'm*. The apostrophe is needed only if a letter is left out.
- Introductory elements in a sentence should be followed by a comma. (Introductory elements include clauses, phrases, and introductory words like *yes, no, oh,* etc.)
- Don't use symbols like "&" in formal writing. Spell out *and*.

Washing the Dog

A young boy, about eight years old, was at the corner grocery store. Picking out a large box of laundry detergent. The grocer a friendly guy asked the boy if he had alot of laundry to do.

"No," the boy said. "I'm going too wash my dog."

"But you shouldn't use this too wash your dog. Its very powerful, if you wash your dog in this, he'll get sick. In fact, it might even kill him."

But the boy was determined. He carried the detergent to the counter. And paid for it.

About a week later the boy came back in the store to by some candy. The grocer asked the boy how his dog was doing. "Oh, he died," the boy said.

The grocer sighed and said he was sorry the dog died. He couldn't help adding, "I told you not to use detergent on your dog."

"I don't think it was the detergent that killed him," said the boy.

"Oh? What was it then?"

"I think it was the spin cycle."

POSSIBLE CORRECTION:

A young boy, about eight years old, was at the corner grocery store picking out a large box of laundry detergent. The grocer, a friendly guy, asked the boy if he had a lot of laundry to do.

"No," the boy said. "I'm going to wash my dog."

"But you shouldn't use this to wash your dog. It's very powerful. If you wash your dog in this, he'll get sick. In fact, it might even kill him."

But the boy was determined. He carried the detergent to the counter and paid for it.

About a week later the boy came back in the store to buy some candy. The grocer asked the boy how his dog was doing. "Oh, he died," the boy said.

The grocer sighed and said he was sorry the dog died. He couldn't help adding, "I told you not to use detergent on your dog."

"I don't think it was the detergent that killed him," said the boy.

"Oh? What was it then?"

"I think it was the spin cycle."

NOTES:

- An appositive should be set off by commas. An appositive breaks the flow of the sentence to give more information about a noun. (Example: *The grocer, a friendly guy, asked the boy if he had a lot of laundry to do.*)
- A comma should not be used to separate two sentences. Use a period, a semicolon, or a comma with *and, but, or, for* or *nor*.
- Many sentence fragments occur simply because the writer has separated a phrase or clause from the rest of a sentence. (Example: *A young boy, about eight years old, was at the corner grocery store. Picking out a large box of laundry detergent.* Corrected: *A young boy, about eight years old, was at the corner grocery store, picking out a large box of laundry detergent.*)
- *A lot* is two words, not one.

Getting Ahead

A young man asked a old rich man how he made his money. The old man said "It was 1932, and I was down to my last nickle. I invested that nickle in a apple. I spent the entire day polishing the apple. At the end of the day, I sold the apple for ten cents. "The next morning, I used the ten cents too buy two apples. I spent the entire day polishing them and sold them at the end of the day for 20 cents. I continued this system for a month. At the end of the month, I had earned $137.00 which was a fortune. So that's how you got rich? the boy asked. "Heavens, no!" the man replied. "Then my wife's uncle died and left us five million dollars."

POSSIBLE CORRECTION:

A young man asked an old rich man how he made his money. The old man said, "It was 1932, and I was down to my last nickel. I invested that nickel in an apple. I spent the entire day polishing the apple. At the end of the day, I sold the apple for ten cents. The next morning, I used the ten cents to buy two apples. I spent the entire day polishing them and sold them at the end of the day for 20 cents. I continued this system for a month. At the end of the month, I had earned $137.00, which was a fortune."

"So that's how you got rich?" the boy asked.

"Heavens, no!" the man replied. "Then my wife's uncle died and left us five million dollars."

NOTES:
- Use *an*, not *a*, before a word that begins with a vowel sound (*an old rich man*).
- When writing dialogue, start a new paragraph with each change of speakers.

Vice Presidency

Tom was excited about his promotion to Vice President of the company he worked for and kept bragging about it to his wife. Finally she couldn't take it any longer, and said "This is not such a big deal. Vice presidents are a dime a dozen. They even have a vice president of peas at the grocery store." Not sure if this was true or not, Tom decided to call the grocery store. A clerk answers and Tom says "Can I please talk to the Vice President of peas?" The clerk replies "Canned or frozen?"

POSSIBLE CORRECTION:

Tom was excited about his promotion to vice president of the company he worked for and kept bragging about it to his wife. Finally, she couldn't take it any longer and said, "This is not such a big deal. Vice presidents are a dime a dozen. They even have a vice president of peas at the grocery store."

Not sure if this was true or not, Tom decided to call the grocery store. A clerk answered and Tom asked, "May I please talk to the vice president of peas?"

The clerk replied, "Canned or frozen?"

NOTES:
- Titles like *president*, *vice president*, and *captain* are capitalized only if they are used as part of the person's name. (Example: *He talked to Vice President Gonzales.*)
- The writer switches from past to present tense near the end of the story. Since the story began in past tense, it should remain in past tense.

Beware of Dog

Outside a little country store, a stranger noticed a sign saying, "DANGER! BEWARE OF DOG!" posted on the glass door. Nervously he went inside and saw an old mutt asleep on the floor beside the cash register. He asked the store manager, "Is *that* the dog folks are supposed to beware of?"

"Thats right," she replied.

The stranger chuckled. "That certainly doesn't look like a dangerous dog to me" he said. Why in the world would you post that sign?"

"Because," the owner replied, "before I posted that sign, people kept triping over him."

POSSIBLE CORRECTION:

Outside a little country store, a stranger noticed a sign saying, "DANGER! BEWARE OF DOG!" posted on the glass door. Nervously, he went inside and saw an old mutt asleep on the floor beside the cash register. He asked the store manager, "Is *that* the dog folks are supposed to beware of?"

"That's right," she replied.

The stranger chuckled. "That certainly doesn't look like a dangerous dog to me," he said. "Why in the world would you post that sign?"

"Because," the owner replied, "before I posted that sign, people kept tripping over him."

NOTES:
- Quotation marks come in pairs. Use them at the beginning *and* at the end of a quotation.
- Indicate a new paragraph by indenting it.
- *That's right* needs an apostrophe because it is a contraction of *that is right*.
- For one-syllable words ending in a consonant preceded by a vowel, the consonant is generally doubled when adding "ed" or "ing" (*tripped, tripping*).

Johnny and the Elephants

Little johnny thot his Big sister new everything. He went up to her and asked, "why do Elephants have trunks."

"They would look silly with glove compartments," she siad.

"Well I have another queschun for you," he said. How do you tell if there is an elephant in your refrigerator?"

She didn't hesitate. "Look for his footprints in the jello"

Little johnny was impressed. "how do you tell if there are two elephants in your refrigerator." He asked.

"Look for two sets of footprints side by side." Answered his sister.

"Alright," siad johnny. "how do you tell if there are three elephants in your refrigerator?"

"The door won't close."

POSSIBLE CORRECTION:

Little Johnny thought his big sister knew everything. He went up to her and asked, "Why do elephants have trunks?"

"They would look silly with glove compartments," she said.

"Well, I have another question for you," he said. "How do you tell if there is an elephant in your refrigerator?"

She didn't hesitate. "Look for his footprints in the Jell-O."

Little Johnny was impressed. "How do you tell if there are two elephants in your refrigerator?" he asked.

"Look for two sets of footprints side by side," answered his sister.

"All right," said Johnny. "How do you tell if there are three elephants in your refrigerator?"

"The door won't close."

NOTES:

This is a good exercise for reviewing a variety of errors.

Elephant Protection

A old man in france got up at five in the morning every singel day. Then he would go out and sprinkel white powder on the rodes.

Finally a little girl approached the man and said "what is it that you are sprinkeling on the rodes." "Its elephant repellent," said the old man. "But everybody noes there are no elephants in france!" said the little girl. The old Man shruged his showlders. "I guess it must be working then!"

POSSIBLE CORRECTION:

An old man in France got up at five in the morning every single day. Then he would go out and sprinkle white powder on the roads.

Finally, a little girl approached the man and said, "What is it that you are sprinkling on the roads?"

"It's elephant repellent," said the old man.

"But everybody knows there are no elephants in France!" said the little girl.

The old man shrugged his shoulders. "I guess it must be working then!"

NOTES:
- Capitalize names of countries.
- Use a question mark at the end of a sentence that asks a question.
- For one-syllable words ending in a consonant preceded by a vowel, the consonant is generally doubled when adding "ed" or "ing" (*shrugged, shrugging*).
- When writing dialogue, start a new paragraph with each change of speakers.

Little Lily's Goldfish

Little Lily was in the garden filling in a whole when her neighbor looked over the fence. He politely asked, "What are you doing Lily?"

"My goldfish died," replied Lily tearfully. "I've just buried him."

The neighbor was concerned. "That's an awfully big hole for a goldfish, isn't it?"

Lily patted down the last heap of earth and then replied, "That's because he's inside you're dumb cat."

POSSIBLE CORRECTION:

Little Lily was in the garden filling in a hole when her neighbor looked over the fence. He politely asked, "What are you doing, Lily?"

"My goldfish died," replied Lily tearfully. "I've just buried him."

The neighbor was concerned. "That's an awfully big hole for a goldfish, isn't it?"

Lily patted down the last heap of earth and then replied, "That's because he's inside your dumb cat."

NOTES:
- *Hole* refers to something in the ground. *Whole* refers to all of something.
- Use a comma before the name at the end of a sentence when you are directly addressing someone (*What are you doing, Lily?*)

The Money or the Daughter

Once there was a millionaire who collected live alligators. He kept them in the pool in back of his mansion. He also had a beautiful daughter. One day he decides to throw a huge party, and during the party he announces, "I have a proposition for every unmarried man here. I will give one million dollars or my daughter to the man who can swim across this pool full of alligators and emerge unharmed." As soon as he finished his last word, there was the sound of a large SPLASH!! Everyone looked into the pool and saw a young man swimming as fast as he could. The crowd cheered him on until he made it to the other side unharmed. The millionaire was impressed. He said, "that was incredible! Fantastic! I didn't think it could be done! Well now you must receive your prize. Which do you want—my daughter or one million dollars?" The young man says, "I don't want your money. And I don't want your daughter. I want the person who pushed me in!"

Possible Correction:

Once there was a millionaire who collected live alligators. He kept them in the pool in back of his mansion. He also had a beautiful daughter.

One day he decided to throw a huge party, and during the party he announced, "I have a proposition for every unmarried man here. I will give one million dollars or my daughter to the man who can swim across this pool full of alligators and emerge unharmed."

As soon as he finished his last word, there was the sound of a large SPLASH!! Everyone looked into the pool and saw a young man swimming as fast as he could. The crowd cheered him on until he made it to the other side unharmed.

The millionaire was impressed. He said, "That was incredible! Fantastic! I didn't think it could be done! Well, now you must receive your prize. Which do you want—my daughter or one million dollars?"

The young man said, "I don't want your money, and I don't want your daughter. I want the person who pushed me in!"

Notes:
- Dividing the story into paragraphs makes it much easier to read.
- Write the story in present tense or past tense. Don't switch back and forth.
- Use a comma after introductory words like *yes, no, oh, well, however,* etc.

Floating a Loan

A banker fell overboard from a friends sailboat. The friend grabbed a life preserver held it up not knowing if the banker could swim and shouted, "Can you float alone?" "Obviously," the banker replied, "but this is a heck of a time to talk business!"

NOTES:
- Use an apostrophe to indicate possession or ownership (*friend's sailboat*).
- Items in a series should be separated with commas.
- When writing dialogue, start a new paragraph with each change of speakers.

Conversation with a Police Officer

An elementery school class went on a field trip to the police station. The Officer pointed to one of the pictures on the "Ten Most Wanted" poster and told the students, "that is the most wanted fugitive in the entire united states."

One student asked. "He is the most wanted in the entire united states?"

The Officer says "Yes."

The student looked at him. Shaking his head in disbelief. "Why didn't you keep him when you took his picture then?"

POSSIBLE CORRECTION:

An elementary school class went on a field trip to the police station. The officer pointed to one of the pictures on the "Ten Most Wanted" poster and told the students, "That is the most wanted fugitive in the entire United States."

One student asked, "He is the most wanted in the entire United States?"

The officer said, "Yes."

The student looked at him, shaking his head in disbelief. "Why didn't you keep him when you took his picture then?"

NOTES:

- Use a comma, in most cases, to separate explanatory material like *he said* from the actual quotation. (Explanatory material can come before or after the quotation. *The officer said* is an example of it coming before.)
- Capitalize titles like officer, captain, vice president, etc. only when they are used with the person's name (*Officer Miller, the officer*).

The Nobel Prize

A women is driving down a country rode when she spots a farmer standing in the middle of a huge field of grass. She pulls the car over too the side of the rode and notices that the farmer is just standing there, doing nothing, looking at nothing. The women gets out of the car, woks all the way out two the farmer and asks, "What are you doing?"

The farmer replies, "I'm trying to when a Nobel Prize."

"How?" asks the woman, puzzled.

"Well I herd they give the Nobel Prize for people out standing in there field."

POSSIBLE CORRECTION:

A woman is driving down a country road when she spots a farmer standing in the middle of a huge field of grass. She pulls the car over to the side of the road and notices that the farmer is just standing there, doing nothing, looking at nothing. The woman gets out of the car, walks all the way out to the farmer and asks, "What are you doing?"

The farmer replies, "I'm trying to win a Nobel Prize."

"How?" asks the woman, puzzled.

"Well, I heard they give the Nobel Prize for people outstanding in their field."

NOTES:

The only errors in this selection are spelling errors that a computer spell check would never catch.

Catching Chickens

The farmers son was returning from the markit with a crate of chickens. All of the sudden the box fell, and broke open. Alot of chickens scurried off in all directions. However the determined boy fixed the crate and walked all over the neighborhood scooping up the birds Hoping he had found them all the boy reluctantly returned home, expecting the worst. "Dad the chicken's got lose," the boy confessed sadly, "but I managed to find all twelve of them".

"you did very well," the farmer smiled. "You left with seven."

POSSIBLE CORRECTION:

The farmer's son was returning from the market with a crate of chickens. All of a sudden, the box fell and broke open. A lot of chickens scurried off in all directions. However, the determined boy fixed the crate and walked all over the neighborhood, scooping up the birds. Hoping he had found them all, the boy reluctantly returned home, expecting the worst. "Dad, the chickens got loose," the boy confessed sadly, "but I managed to find all twelve of them."

"You did very well," the farmer smiled. "You left with seven."

NOTES:

- Use an apostrophe to indicate possession or ownership, as in *the farmer's son*. (The farmer doesn't really possess or own the son, but the phrase is still considered to be possessive since he is "his" son.)
- *All of a sudden* is correct, despite the increasing use of the phrase *all of the sudden*.
- *Lose* and *loose* are frequently confused by writers.
- Periods and commas at the end of a quotation always appear *inside* the quotation marks, not outside.

Biology Test

A professor at a university was giving the final examination for a difficult course. The examination was two hours long, and exam booklets were provided. The professor was very strict and told the class that any exam not on his desk in exactly two hours would not be accepted, and the student would fail. Half an hour into the exam, a student came rushing in and asked the professor for an exam booklet. "You're not going to have time to finish this," the professor said as he handed the student a booklet. "Yes, I will," replied the student. He then took a seat and began writing. After two hours, the professor called for the exams, and the students handed them in—all except the late student, who continued to write. An hour later, that student finished and tried to put his exam on the stack of exam booklets already there. "I'm not going to accept that. It's late," said the professor. The student looked at him angrily and said, "Do you know who I am?" "No, as a matter of fact, I don't," replied the professor sarcastically. "Do you know who I am?" the student repeated in a louder voice. "No, I don't, and I don't care," sniffed the professor. "Good," said the student, who quickly lifted the stack of completed exams, stuffed his in the middle, and walked out of the room.

POSSIBLE CORRECTION:

A professor at a university was giving the final examination for a difficult course. The examination was two hours long, and exam booklets were provided. The professor was very strict and told the class that any exam not on his desk in exactly two hours would not be accepted, and the student would fail.

Half an hour into the exam, a student came rushing in and asked the professor for an exam booklet. "You're not going to have time to finish this," the professor said as he handed the student a booklet.

"Yes, I will," replied the student. He then took a seat and began writing.

After two hours, the professor called for the exams, and the students handed them in—all except the late student, who continued to write. An hour later, that student finished and tried to put his exam on the stack of exam booklets already there.

"I'm not going to accept that. It's late," said the professor.

The student looked at him angrily and said, "Do you know who I am?"

"No, as a matter of fact, I don't," replied the professor sarcastically.

"Do you know who I am?" the student repeated in a louder voice.

"No, I don't, and I don't care," sniffed the professor.

"Good," said the student, who quickly lifted the stack of completed exams, stuffed his in the middle, and walked out of the room.

NOTES:
The only problem with the original is the lack of paragraphing.

Expectant Fathers

For expectant fathers were in a hospital weighting room, while they're wives were in labor. The nurse arrived and announced to the first man, "Congratulations, sir. Your the father of twins."

"Wonderful!" exclaimed the man. "What a coincidence. I work for the Minnesota Twins baseball teem."

The nurse returned in a little while and said to the second man, "Congratulations! Your the father of triplets."

"Wonderful!" he exclaimed. "This is even more of a coincidence. I work for 3M."

An our later, the nurse came back. This time, she turned to the third man. "Congratulations, sir," she said. "You're wife just gave birth to quadruplets."

The pour man was flabbergasted. He couldn't say a thing.

"Don't tell me," said the nurse. "Another coincidence?"

After the man recovered a bit from the shock, he said, "Yes. I work for the Four Seasons Hotel."

Suddenly the forth guy fainted and fell too the floor. The nurse rushed to his sighed. When he finally regained consciousness, she asked, "Sir, are ewe all right?"

"Yes," he said. "I just had a shocking thought. I work at 7-11."

POSSIBLE CORRECTION:

Four expectant fathers were in a hospital waiting room while their wives were in labor. The nurse arrived and announced to the first man, "Congratulations, sir. You're the father of twins."

"Wonderful!" exclaimed the man. "What a coincidence. I work for the Minnesota Twins baseball team."

The nurse returned in a little while and said to the second man, "Congratulations! You're the father of triplets."

"Wonderful!" he exclaimed. "This is even more of a coincidence. I work for 3M."

An hour later, the nurse came back. This time, she turned to the third man. "Congratulations, sir," she said. "Your wife just gave birth to quadruplets."

The poor man was flabbergasted. He couldn't say a thing.

"Don't tell me," said the nurse. "Another coincidence?"

After the man recovered a bit from the shock, he said, "Yes. I work for the Four Seasons Hotel."

Suddenly the fourth guy fainted and fell to the floor. The nurse rushed to his side. When he finally regained consciousness, she asked, "Sir, are you all right?"

"Yes," he said. "I just had a shocking thought. I work at 7-11."

NOTES:

The only mistakes in the original are spelling errors that a computer spell check would never catch.

Chocolate Covered Peanuts

Scott went to visit his aunt in the hospital, he found her taking a nap. He sat down in a chair in her room, fliped threw a few magazines, and munched on sum peanuts in a bowl on the table. Eventualy, the aunt woke up, her nephew realized he had absentmindedly finished the entire bowl. "I'm sorry, aunt elizabeth," he said. "I see Ive eaten all of your peanuts." "That's okay Scott," the aunt replied. "After Ive sucked the chocolate off, I don't like them much any way."

POSSIBLE CORRECTION:

When Scott went to visit his aunt in the hospital, he found her taking a nap. He sat down in a chair in her room, flipped through a few magazines, and munched on some peanuts in a bowl on the table. Eventually, the aunt woke up, and her nephew realized he had absentmindedly finished the entire bowl. "I'm sorry, Aunt Elizabeth," he said. "I see I've eaten all of your peanuts!"

"That's okay, Scott," the aunt replied. "After I've sucked the chocolate off, I don't like them much anyway."

NOTES:

- A comma should not be used to separate two sentences. Use a period, a semicolon, or a comma with *and, but, or, for* or *nor*. Another approach is to rewrite so that you no longer have two complete sentences. (No: *Scott went to visit his aunt in the hospital, he found her taking a nap.* Yes: **When** *Scott went to visit his aunt in the hospital, he found her taking a nap.*)
- For one-syllable words ending in a consonant preceded by a vowel, the consonant is generally doubled when adding "ed" or "ing" (*flipped, flipping*).
- Use a comma to set off a person's name when directly addressing the person. (Examples: *That's okay, Joseph. Joseph, that's okay. That, Joseph, is okay.*)

Japanese Banking Crisis

According to inside contacts, there is no relief in sight for the recent Japanese banking crisis. If anything, it's getting worse. Following last week's news that Origami Bank folded, newspapers reported that Sumo Bank has now gone belly up, and Bonsai Bank plans to cut back some of its branches. Karaoke Bank is up for sale, and it is going for a song. Meanwhile, shares in Kamikaze Bank have nose-dived, and analysts report that there is something fishy going on at Sushi Bank. Staff members there fear they may get a raw deal.

POSSIBLE CORRECTION:

According to inside contacts, there is no relief in sight for the recent Japanese banking crisis. If anything, it's getting worse. Following last week's news that Origami Bank folded, newspapers reported that Sumo Bank has now gone belly up, and Bonsai Bank plans to cut back some of its branches. Karaoke Bank is up for sale, and it is going for a song. Meanwhile, shares in Kamikaze Bank have nose-dived, and analysts report that there is something fishy going on at Sushi Bank. Staff members there fear they may get a raw deal.

NOTES:

You may want to keep your students on their toes by throwing in a story with *no* errors. This is one of them.

Eating Caterpillars

"Daddy are caterpillars good to eat" asked little Emily.

"I told you not to mention such things during meals. Now eat your dinner" said her Father.

Emily's Mother was a bit more patient. "Why did you ask that Emily," she asked.

"Its because I saw one on daddy's lettuce," Emily said. "Now its gone.

POSSIBLE CORRECTION:

"Daddy, are caterpillars good to eat?" asked little Emily.

"I told you not to mention such things during meals. Now eat your dinner," said her father.

Emily's mother was a bit more patient. "Why did you ask that, Emily?" she asked.

"It's because I saw one on Daddy's lettuce," Emily said. "Now it's gone."

NOTES:
- Use a comma to set off a person's name when someone is directly addressing that person. (In this case, the child is using *Daddy* as his name.)
- Apostrophes can be used to show possession or ownership, as in *Daddy's lettuce.* They can also be used to indicate a missing letter, as in *it's gone.*

Frozen Turkeys

A woman picking through the frozen turkeys' at the grocery store. Couldn't find one big enough for her family of eight. She asks a stock boy, "Do those turkey's get any bigger?"

The stock boy replied, "No ma'am. their dead."

NOTES:

This short piece includes a sentence fragment, unnecessary apostrophes, a change in tenses, and a misspelled word.

Four Psychiatrists

A group of psychiatrists was attending a convention. Four of them were talking in a restraunt. One said, "People are always coming to us with their guilt & fears, but we have no one that we can go to when we have problems." The others agreed.

Than one said, "Since we are all professionals, why don't we take some time write now to here each other out?"

The other three agreed. The first then confesses, "I have an uncontrolable desire to make fun of my patients." The second psychiatrist said, "I love expensive things. I find ways to cheat my patients out of their money whenever I can so I can buy the things I want." The third psychiatrist said, "I'am involved with selling drugs & often get my patients to sell them for me." The fourth psychiatrist then confessed, "I know I'am suppose too, but no matter how hard I try, I can't keep a secret."

Possible Correction:

A group of psychiatrists was attending a convention. Four of them were talking in a restaurant. One said, "People are always coming to us with their guilt and fears, but we have no one that we can go to when we have problems." The others agreed.

Then one said, "Since we are all professionals, why don't we take some time right now to hear each other out?"

The other three agreed. The first then confessed, "I have an uncontrollable desire to make fun of my patients."

The second psychiatrist said, "I love expensive things. I find ways to cheat my patients out of their money whenever I can so I can buy the things I want."

The third psychiatrist said, "I'm involved with selling drugs and often get my patients to sell them for me."

The fourth psychiatrist then confessed, "I know I'm supposed to, but no matter how hard I try, I can't keep a secret."

NOTES:
- Since the story starts out in past tense, it should remain in past tense.
- When writing dialogue, start a new paragraph with each change of speakers.
- In the second paragraph, *write* should be *right*, and *here* should be *hear*.
- *I'am* should be *I am* or *I'm*.
- Don't use symbols like "&" in formal writing. Spell out *and*.
- *Suppose too* should be *supposed to*. Students often forget the "d" because they don't hear it.

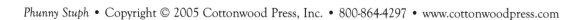

Listening to Father

A minister walking down a country lane sees a young farmer. Struggling to load hay back onto a cart. "You look hot, my son". said the minister. "Rest a moment and let me give you a hand."

"No thanks." Said the young man. "My father wouldn't like it."

"I'm sure he wouldn't mind," the minister said. "Everyone is entitled to a brake. Come and have a drink of water." Again the young man said that his father would be upset.

Loosing his patience, the minister said, "Your father must be a real slave driver. I'd like to give him a piece of my mind. Tell me where I can find him!"

"Well", replied the young farmer, "look down. He's under the load of hey."

POSSIBLE CORRECTION:

A minister walking down a country lane sees a young farmer struggling to load hay back onto a cart. "You look hot, my son," said the minister. "Rest a moment and let me give you a hand."

"No, thanks," said the young man. "My father wouldn't like it."

"I'm sure he wouldn't mind," the minister said. "Everyone is entitled to a break. Come and have a drink of water." Again, the young man said that his father would be upset.

Losing his patience, the minister said, "Your father must be a real slave driver. I'd like to give him a piece of my mind. Tell me where I can find him!"

"Well," replied the young farmer, "look down. He's under the load of hay."

NOTES:
- Many sentence fragments are formed simply because a period is placed too soon. (Example: *A minister walking down a country lane sees a young farmer. Struggling to load hay back onto a cart.*)
- Commas and periods should be placed *before* the quotation marks at the end of a quotation, not after.
- Use a comma after introductory words like *yes, no, oh, well,* etc.

Grandma's Home

When the bus driver stopped to pick up Angela for preschool, he noticed an older women hugging her as she left the house. "Is that your Grandmother?" the Bus Driver asked.

"Yes," Angela said. "She's come to visit us for christmas."

"How nice," said the Bus Driver. "Where does she live?"

"At the Airport," Angela said. "Whenever we want her, we just go out there and get her."

When the bus driver stopped to pick up Angela for pre-school, he noticed an older woman hugging her as she left the house. "Is that your grandmother?" the bus driver asked.

"Yes," Angela said. "She's come to visit us for Christmas."

"How nice," said the bus driver. "Where does she live?"

"At the airport," Angela said. "Whenever we want her, we just go out there and get her."

NOTES:

This is a good exercise for reviewing capitalization rules. Many students mistakenly capitalize many ordinary nouns.

Emotional Extremes

Some future psychiatrists were attending there first class on human emotions. The professor turned to a student from oregon. "What is the opposite of joy?" he asked.

"Sadness," said the student.

What is the opposite of depression?" he asked a student from new york.

"Elation," she said.

He turned to a student from Texas. "what is the opposite of woe?" he asked.

The texan replied, "sir, I believe that would be giddy-up.

POSSIBLE CORRECTION:

Some future psychiatrists were attending their first class on human emotions. The professor turned to a student from Oregon. "What is the opposite of joy?" he asked.

"Sadness," said the student.

"What is the opposite of depression?" he asked a student from New York.

"Elation," she said.

He turned to a student from Texas. "What is the opposite of woe?" he asked.

The Texan replied, "Sir, I believe that would be giddy-up."

NOTES:
- Capitalize the names of states and words made from the names of states (*Texas* and *Texan).*
- Quotation marks come in pairs. Use them at the beginning *and* at the end of the quotation.

Trusted Employee

A wealthy invester walked into a bank and said to the bank manager, "I would like to speak with Mr. Reginald Jones. I understood he is a tried and trusted employee of yours." The banker goes, "Yes he certainly was trusted, and he will be tried—as soon as we catch him."

POSSIBLE CORRECTION:

A wealthy investor walked into a bank and said to the bank manager, "I would like to speak with Mr. Reginald Jones. I understand he is a tried and trusted employee of yours."

The banker replied, "Yes, he certainly was trusted, and he will be tried—as soon as we catch him."

NOTES:
- Though many people use it informally, *goes* should not be substituted for *said*.
- When writing dialogue, start a new paragraph with each change of speakers.
- Use a comma after introductory words like *yes, no, oh, well,* etc.

The Old Man and the Drummers

A wise old gentlemen retired and bought a home near a Middle School. He spent a quiet Summer in his knew home and then the school year begins, and his peace and quite came to a sudden halt.

On the first day of school three boys came down. The alley beating marrily on every trash can they see, and the same thing happens the next day and the next, and the noise started driving the wise old man crazy. Time for action.

The next afternoon he stops the drummers as they banged their way down the street. He says, "You kids are alot of fun! I love hearing your drumming, because it is so cheerful, and it reminds me of what I use to do at your age, will you do me a favor?"

The boys looked at him suspisiously. "What?" they ask.

"I'll give you a doller if you promise to come around every single day and keep beating on those trash cans," said the man.

The boys was thrilled. Everyday they pounded on trash cans and collected a doller.

After about a week, the wise old man stops the boys again and this time he looked a little bit sad, I still love you're drumming, he said to the boys. However I'm afraid spending a dollar a day is hard on me, I'am on a fixed income. From now on, I'm only going to be able too pay you 50 sense to beat on the cans.

The boys weren't to happy, but they decided to except 50 cents a day, and they continued beating on all the trash cans.

After another week the clever old man stopped the boys again. "I've got more bad news," he said. "My Social Security check hasn't come yet, so I'm not going to be able to give you more than 25 cents a day. Is that all right"

"Are you kidding?" said one of the boys. "Were not going to waist our time beating on those trash cans four only a lousy quarter! We quit!
The wise old man smiled and enjoyed his peace and quite.

POSSIBLE CORRECTION:

A wise old gentleman retired and bought a home near a middle school. He spent a quiet summer in his new home. Then the school year began, and his peace and quiet came to a sudden halt.

On the first day of school, three boys came down the alley, beating merrily on every trash can they saw. The same thing happened the next day and the next, and the noise started driving the wise old man crazy. He decided it was time for action.

The next afternoon, he stopped the drummers as they banged their way down the street. He said, "You kids are a lot of fun! I love hearing your drumming because it is so cheerful, and it reminds me of what I used to do at your age. Will you do me a favor?"

The boys looked at him suspiciously. "What?" they asked.

"I'll give you a dollar if you promise to come around every single day and keep beating on those trash cans," said the man.

The boys were thrilled. Every day they pounded on trash cans and collected a dollar.

After about a week, the wise old man stopped the boys again. This time he looked a little bit sad. "I still love your drumming," he said to the boys. "However, I'm afraid spending a dollar a day is hard on me because I am on a fixed income. From now on, I'm only going to be able to pay you 50 cents to beat on the cans."

The boys weren't too happy, but they decided to accept 50 cents a day. They continued beating on all the trash cans.

After another week the clever old man stopped the boys again. "I've got more bad news," he said. "My Social Security check hasn't come yet, so I'm not going to be able to give you more than 25 cents a day. Is that all right?"

"Are you kidding?" said one of the boys. "We're not going to waste our time beating on those trash cans for only a lousy quarter! We quit!"

The wise old man smiled and enjoyed his peace and quiet.

NOTES:

This story has many errors of many kinds, including spelling errors, run-on sentences, sentence fragments, tense shifts, subject/verb agreement. It is a good one to use when you really want to challenge your students.

A Gift for the Teacher

A kindergarden teacher was opening gifts from her students at the end of the school year. First the florists son handed her a gift. She shook it and smelled it. Then she said, I know what it is: flowers."

That's right," the boy said. "how did you know?"

"Oh it was just a wild guess," she said.

The next pupil was the candy shop owners daughter. The teacher held the gift up smelled it shook it and said, "I'll bet I can guess what this is, it's a box of candy.

"That's right," the girl said. "how did you know?"

"Oh it was just a wild guess," said the teacher.

The next gift was from the restaurant owners son. The teacher held the package overhead but it was leaking. She touched a drop of the leakage with her finger and then she touched it to her tongue.

"Is it Seven-Up?" she asked.

"No," the boy replied, with some excitement.

The teacher repeated the process, taking a larger drop of the leakage to her tongue. Is it apple juice?" she asked.

"No," the boy replied, with more excitement.

The teacher took one more taste. Then she said, "I give up, what is it?

The little boy smiled, he was thrilled to have fooled her. "It's a puppy!" he cried.

Possible Correction:

A kindergarten teacher was opening gifts from her students at the end of the school year. First, the florist's son handed her a gift. She shook it and smelled it. Then she said, "I know what it is: flowers."

"That's right," the boy said. "How did you know?"

"Oh, it was just a wild guess," she said.

The next pupil was the candy shop owner's daughter. The teacher held the gift up, smelled it, shook it, and said, "I'll bet I can guess what this is. It's a box of candy."

"That's right," the girl said. "How did you know?"

"Oh, it was just a wild guess," said the teacher.

The next gift was from the restaurant owner's son. The teacher held the package overhead, but it was leaking. She touched a drop of the leakage with her finger, and then she touched it to her tongue.

"Is it Seven-Up?" she asked.

"No," the boy replied, with some excitement.

The teacher repeated the process, taking a larger drop of the leakage to her tongue. "Is it apple juice?" she asked.

"No," the boy replied, with more excitement.

The teacher took one more taste. Then she said, "I give up. What is it?"

The little boy smiled. He was thrilled to have fooled her. "It's a puppy!" he cried.

NOTES:
- Use an apostrophe to indicate "possession" (*florist's son, candy shop owner's daughter, restaurant owner's son*).
- Introductory words like *yes, no, oh, well,* etc., should be followed by a comma.
- Items in a series should be separated with commas (*held the gift up, smelled it, shook it, and said...*)
- Quotation marks come in pairs. Use them at the beginning *and* at the end of the quotation.
- A comma is needed with the conjunction in a compound sentence. (*The teacher held the package overhead,* **but** *it was leaking. She touched a drop of the leakage with her finger,* **and** *then she touched it to her tongue.*)
- A comma should not be used to separate two sentences. Use a period or a semicolon. (No: *I give up, what is it?* Yes: *I give up. What is it?*)

Boots

"Can you help me put on my boots? a kindergartner asked.

"Sure," says his teacher, she could see he was having trouble. Even with her pulling and him pushing, the boots still didn't want to go on. By the time the second boot was on the boys foot, the teacher had worked up quiet a sweat.

Then the little boy said, Mrs. Williams, their on the wrong feet." She looked down. They were.

It wasn't any easier pulling the boots off, but she finally managed. Then she pulled, and he pushed some more. Together, they managed to get the boots back on. This time they were on the right feet.

Then the little boy said, "These aren't my boots.

The teacher took a deep breathe. She wanted to yell, but she didn't. Once again, she pulled the boots off. By now she was dripping with sweat and a little out of breath.

Then the boy said, "There my brother's boots. My Mom made me wear them today."

The teacher didn't know if she should laugh or cry. Somehow she found the strength to pull the boots on the boys feet again. She sighed. Then she asked, Now where are your mittens?

He said, "I stuffed them in the toes of my boots..."

POSSIBLE CORRECTION:

"Can you help me put on my boots?" a kindergartner asked.

"Sure," said his teacher. She could see he was having trouble. Even with her pulling and him pushing, the boots still didn't want to go on. By the time the second boot was on the boy's foot, the teacher had worked up quite a sweat.

Then the little boy said, "Mrs. Williams, they're on the wrong feet." She looked down. They were.

It wasn't any easier pulling the boots off, but she finally managed. Then she pulled, and he pushed some more. Together, they managed to get the boots back on. This time they were on the right feet.

Then the little boy said, "These aren't my boots."

The teacher took a deep breath. She wanted to yell, but she didn't. Once again, she pulled the boots off. By now she was dripping with sweat and a little out of breath.

Then the boy said, "They're my brother's boots. My mom made me wear them today."

The teacher didn't know if she should laugh or cry. Somehow, she found the strength to pull the boots on the boy's feet again. She sighed. Then she asked, "Now, where are your mittens?"

He said, "I stuffed them in the toes of my boots..."

NOTES:

- Quotation marks come in pairs. Use them at the beginning *and* at the end of the quotation.
- Use an apostrophe to indicate possession (*boy's foot*).
- *They're* is a contraction of *they are*. Use *they're* when *they are* can be substituted in a sentence.
- Use a comma to set off a person's name when someone is directly addressing that person (*Mrs. Williams, they're on the wrong feet.*)
- "Mom" is not capitalized unless it is being used instead of the person's name, as a noun of direct address. Therefore, the word should not be capitalized in *my mom*.

Help Wanted

A dog troted up to a window in an office & seen a sign that said, "HELP WANTED. Must be able to type. Must be good with a computer. Must be bilingual. We are an Equal Opportunity Employer."

The dog went inside looked at the Office Manager wagged his tale walked over to the sign looked at it and whined. Getting the idea, the Manager said, "I can't hire you. The sign says you have to be able to type."

The dog troted over to the computer & typed out a perfect letter and printed it. He gave it to the manager and jumped up on a chair.

The manager was stunned, but then she told the dog, "The sign says you have to be good with a computer. Just cuz you can type doesn't mean you are good with computers."

The dog jumped down and troted back to the computor. This time he opened PhotoShop designed a color flyer and printed it out.

By this time, the manager was in shock. Finally she sighed looked at the dog and said, "You are clearly a very intelligent dog with some useful job skills, however I can't give you the job."

The dog jumped down troted over to the sign in the window and put his paw on the words "Equal Opportunity Employer."

"Yes, I see that," said the Manager, "but the sign *also* says "Must be bilingual."

The dog looked at the manager calmly and said, "Meow!"

122

Possible Correction:

A dog trotted up to a window in an office and saw a sign that said, "HELP WANTED. Must be able to type. Must be good with a computer. Must be bilingual. We are an Equal Opportunity Employer."

The dog went inside, looked at the office manager, wagged his tail, walked over to the sign, looked at it, and whined. Getting the idea, the manager said, "I can't hire you. The sign says you have to be able to type."

The dog trotted over to the computer, typed out a perfect letter, and printed it. He gave it to the manager and jumped up on a chair.

The manager was stunned, but then she told the dog, "The sign says you have to be good with a computer. Just because you can type doesn't mean you are good with computers."

The dog jumped down and trotted back to the computer. This time he opened Photoshop, designed a color flyer, and printed it out.

By this time, the manager was in shock. Finally, she sighed, looked at the dog, and said, "You are clearly a very intelligent dog with some useful job skills. However, I can't give you the job."

The dog jumped down, trotted over to the sign in the window, and put his paw on the words "Equal Opportunity Employer."

"Yes, I see that," said the manager, "but the sign *also* says 'Must be bilingual.'"

The dog looked at the manager calmly and said, "Meow!"

Notes:

- Items in a series must be separated by commas.
- There is no need to capitalize *office manager*. It is just the name of a job, like *cook, airline pilot,* or *teacher.*
- For one-syllable words ending in a consonant preceded by a vowel, the consonant is generally doubled when adding "ed" or "ing" (*trotted, trotting*).
- When a quotation includes another quotation, put single quotation marks around the second quotation (*"but the sign also says, 'Must be bilingual.'"*)
- Don't use symbols like "&" in formal writing. Spell out *and.*
- *Cuz* should be spelled *because.*

Centipede

A man walked into a pet shop. "I want to buy a pet that can do everything," he said.

"How about a dog?" asked the shop owner.

"No. A dog can't do everything."

"Alright, how about a cat?"

"No way! A cat can't do everything. I want a pet that can do everything!" insisted the man.

The shop owner thought for a minute and then said, "I've got it! A centipede!"

The man was skeptical, but he decided to try one out. He chose a centipede and took it home. "Clean the kitchen!" he demanded. Then he went to take a nap. Thirty minutes later, he walked into an immaculate kitchen. The dishes were all washed, dried and put away. The appliances sparkled, and the floor gleamed. The man was amazed.

He told the centipede to clean the living room. Twenty minutes later, he walked in to find the carpet had been vacuumed, the furniture dusted, and the plants watered. The man was amazed.

He decided to try one more thing. "Run down to the corner and get me a newspaper," he said. The centipede walked out the door.

Ten minutes passed, and the centipede did not return. Twenty minutes passed, and then thirty. The centipede did not appear.

By this point, the man was wondering what had happened. He went to the front door, opened it, and found the centipede sitting right outside.

"What's wrong with you?" asked the man. "I sent you down to the store over thirty minutes ago. What's the matter?"

"I'm going! I'm going!" said the centipede. I'm just putting on my shoes!"

POSSIBLE CORRECTION:

A man walked into a pet shop. "I want to buy a pet that can do everything," he said.

"How about a dog?" asked the shop owner.

"No. A dog can't do everything."

"All right, how about a cat?"

"No way! A cat can't do everything. I want a pet that can do everything!" insisted the man.

The shop owner thought for a minute and then said, "I've got it! A centipede!"

The man was skeptical, but he decided to try one out. He chose a centipede and took it home. "Clean the kitchen!" he demanded. Then he went to take a nap. Thirty minutes later, he walked into an immaculate kitchen. The dishes were all washed, dried and put away. The appliances sparkled, and the floor gleamed. The man was amazed.

He told the centipede to clean the living room. Twenty minutes later, he walked in to find the carpet had been vacuumed, the furniture dusted, and the plants watered. The man was amazed.

He decided to try one more thing. "Run down to the corner and get me a newspaper," he said. The centipede walked out the door.

Ten minutes passed, and the centipede did not return. Twenty minutes passed, and then thirty. The centipede did not appear.

By this point, the man was wondering what had happened. He went to the front door, opened it, and found the centipede sitting right outside.

"What's wrong with you?" asked the man. "I sent you down to the store over thirty minutes ago. What's the matter?"

"I'm going! I'm going!" said the centipede. I'm just putting on my shoes!"

NOTES:

This exercise contains only one error. *Alright* is spelled incorrectly. It should be spelled as two words: *all right*.

Dead Dog

Mr. Jones took his dead dog to the veterinarian. He said "I think my dog is reel sick. Would you please examine him and tell me what you think?"

The vet looked at the dog and says "I'm very sorry Mr. Jones, but your dog has dyed." "Are you sure doctor fazio? Is there any tests you can run to be sure" the man begged.

"Well okay" said the doctor. She turned to her assistant and said "Please bring me Fluffy"

The assistant brought in the office cat. Fluffy proceeded to sniff the dog from nose to tail. Then she jumped off the table and left.

"That confirms my diagnosis, Mr. Jones" says the doctor. "Your dog has definitely passed on. Theres more bad news, to. I'm afraid I'm going to have to bill you for our services." She handed Mr. Jones a bill. "Are you crazy" cried Mr. Jones, looking at the bill "Three hundred dollars to tell me my dog is dead?"

"No" said doctor fazio. "That part was only $25.00. The other $275.00 was for the cat scan."

Possible Correction:

Mr. Jones took his dead dog to the veterinarian. He said, "I think my dog is real sick. Would you please examine him and tell me what you think?"

The vet looked at the dog and said, "I'm very sorry, Mr. Jones, but your dog has died."

"Are you sure, Doctor Fazio? Are there any tests you can run to be sure?" the man begged.

"Well, okay," said the doctor. She turned to her assistant and said, "Please bring me Fluffy."

The assistant brought in the office cat. Fluffy proceeded to sniff the dog from nose to tail. Then she jumped off the table and left.

"That confirms my diagnosis, Mr. Jones," said the doctor. "Your dog has definitely passed on. There's more bad news, too. I'm afraid I'm going to have to bill you for our services." She handed Mr. Jones a bill.

"Are you crazy?" cried Mr. Jones, looking at the bill. "Three hundred dollars to tell me my dog is dead?"

"No," said Doctor Fazio. "That part was only $25.00. The other $275.00 was for the cat scan."

NOTES:

- The story starts out in past tense. It should stay in past tense.
- Use a comma to set off a noun of direct address. (*I'm very sorry, Mr. Jones, but your dog has died.*)
- *Dyed* refers to pigments. *Died* is the word needed in the second paragraph.
- When writing dialogue, start a new paragraph with each change of speakers.

Backseat Driver

an urban legend

This is really true, so you really ought to pay attention because it really happened to a friend of my girlfriends mother and its a pretty good warning for any woman who is driving alone at night, and the night this happened, it was dark and foggy and the lady, who's name was Denise, was having trouble staying awake, and besides that the road was slick and she was running low on gas and didn't know where the next town was and she was afraid she was going to have to pull over and sleep by the side of the road until morning. Just then she saw a little run-down gas station, and she pulled in too get gas and pulled out her credit card and started to pump when an attendant came out and started acting weird and making faces at her and this really freaked her out exspecially when he said he "smelled trouble" and asked her to pop open her hood and she didn't want too and was so worried about being in the middle of nowhere and having this creepy gas station attendant finding reasons to keep her there. Finally he said he wanted to show her something under the hood, and even though she didn't want to, for some reason she did as he asked and as she came around to the front of the car he grabbed her arm and said "This car needs a tow, you'll have to come with me to the office," and he put his hand over her mouth and forced her into the office, and she was really scared then and tried to bite his hand, and when they got inside, he said, "I'm sorry, but there is a man crouched down in the backseat of your car and I didn't want him to know that I'd seen him," so you can imagine how she felt then, and they called the police and they came and found a serial killer in the back of her car where he had somehow stowed away and was just waiting to add her to his list of victims, and the best part of the story is that Denise married the gas station attendant and now the two of them own the station and their three kids help them with the chores.

POSSIBLE CORRECTION:

This is really true, so you really ought to pay attention. It really happened to a friend of my girlfriend's mother, and it's a pretty good warning for any woman who is driving alone at night to be careful.

The night this happened, it was dark and foggy. Denise was having trouble staying awake. Besides that, the road was slick, and she was running low on gas. She didn't know where the next town was, and she was afraid she was going to have to pull over and sleep by the side of the road until morning. Just then she saw a little run-down gas station, and she pulled in to get gas. She pulled out her credit card and started to pump when an attendant came out and started acting weird and making faces at her. This really freaked her out, especially when he said he "smelled trouble" and asked her to pop open her hood. She didn't want to. She was so worried about being in the middle of nowhere and having a creepy gas station attendant finding reasons to keep her there.

Finally, he said he wanted to show her something under the hood. Even though she didn't want to, for some reason she did as he asked. As she came around to the front of the car, he grabbed her arm and said, "This car needs a tow. You'll have to come with me to the office." He put his hand over her mouth and forced her into the office. She was really scared then and tried to bite his hand. When they got inside, he said, "I'm sorry, but there is a man crouched down in the backseat of your car. I didn't want him to know that I'd seen him." You can imagine how she felt then. They called the police, and they came and found a serial killer in the back of her car, where he had somehow stowed away and was just waiting to add her to his list of victims.

The best part of the story is that Denise married the gas station attendant. Now the two of them own the station, and their three kids help them with the chores.

NOTES:

Run-on sentences and a lack of paragraphing are clearly the main problems with this story. Of course, there are many ways to correct the piece.

Police Training

It is January 17 2005 and three cadets are training to become police detectives. The sargeant decides to test they're skill at reconizing a suspect. He shows the first cadet a picture for five seconds and then hides it. Then he says, "That was your suspect, how would you recognize him?"

"That's easy, answered the cadet. "We would find him fast because he only has one eye.

The sargeant thinks a minute and then answered, "Well that's because the picture I showed you is a profile. It shows only a side view." He can't believe the cadet has given him such a ridiculous answer, but he goes on to the second cadet. Flashing the picture for five seconds to him. Again he asks, "That was your suspect, how would you recognize him?"

The second cadet smiled and says, "It would be easy too catch, because he has only one ear!"

The police sargeant shakes his head in disbelieve. Then angrily responds, "What's the matter with you two? Of course only one eye and one ear are showing, it's a picture of his profile! Is that the best answer you can come up with?!" Extremely frustrated at this point, he shows the picture to the 3rd cadet and in a very testy voice asks, "This is your suspect. How would you recognize him?" He quickly adds, "Think hard before giving me a stupid answer."

The cadet looks at the picture intently for a moment. Then she says, "The suspect wares contact lenses."

The sargeant is speechless. He goes to his office checks the suspects file in his computer and comes back. He is beaming. "Its true! The suspect does indeed wear contact lenses. Tell us how you were able to make such an astute observation!

"It was easy," said the cadet. "He can't wear glasses because he only has one eye and one ear."

POSSIBLE CORRECTION:

It is January 17, 2005, and three cadets are training to become police detectives. The sergeant decides to test their skill at recognizing a suspect. He shows the first cadet a picture for five seconds and then hides it. Then he says, "That was your suspect. How would you recognize him?"

"That's easy," answers the cadet. "We would find him fast because he only has one eye."

The sergeant thinks a minute and then answers, "Well, that's because the picture I showed you is a profile. It shows only a side view." He can't believe the cadet has given him such a ridiculous answer, but he goes on to the second cadet. Flashing the picture for five seconds to him, again he asks, "That was your suspect. How would you recognize him?"

The second cadet smiles and says, "He would be easy to catch because he has only one ear."

The police sergeant shakes his head in disbelief and then angrily responds, "What's the matter with you two? Of course only one eye and one ear are showing. It's a picture of his profile! Is that the best answer you can come up with?!" Extremely frustrated at this point, he shows the picture to the third cadet and in a very testy voice asks, "This is your suspect. How would you recognize him?" He quickly adds, "Think hard before giving me a stupid answer."

The cadet looks at the picture intently for a moment. Then she says, "The suspect wears contact lenses."

The sergeant is speechless. He goes to his office, checks the suspect's file in his computer and comes back. He is beaming. "It's true! The suspect does indeed wear contact lenses. Tell us how you were able to make such an astute observation!"

"It was easy," says the cadet. "He can't wear glasses because he only has one eye and one ear."

NOTES:

Because it has so many errors of so many kinds, this exercise is a good one to use if you really want to challenge your students.

Hunting Ducks

A duck hunter named Frank searched and searched for the perfect bird dog and he was thrilled to finally find a dog that could actually walk on water to retreive a duck, and he couldn't believe his good luck but he worried that none of his friends would ever believe him so he decided to introduce the dog first to a friend an eternal pessimist who refused to be impressed by anything because he thought surely this dog would impress his freind.

He invited the freind to go hunting with him and his new dog and they waited by the shore and soon a flock of ducks flew by so they fired and a duck fell and the dog jumped into the water but he did not sink, he walked across the water to retreive the bird barely getting his paws wet.

This continued all day long, each time a duck fell the dog walked across the surface of the water to retreive it and the pessimist watched carefully but said nothing and finally on the drive home Frank asked, "Did you notice anything unusual about my new dog?" "Yes," said the pessimist. "He can't swim."

Phunny Stuph • Copyright © 2005 Cottonwood Press, Inc. • 800-864-4297 • www.cottonwoodpress.com
132

POSSIBLE CORRECTION:

A duck hunter named Frank searched and searched for the perfect bird dog. He was thrilled to finally find a dog that could actually walk on water to retrieve a duck. He couldn't believe his good luck, but he worried that none of his friends would ever believe him. He decided to introduce the dog first to a friend, an eternal pessimist who refused to be impressed by anything. He thought surely this dog would impress his friend.

He invited the friend to go hunting with him and his new dog. They waited by the shore, and soon a flock of ducks flew by. They fired, and a duck fell. The dog jumped into the water, but he did not sink. He walked across the water to retrieve the bird, barely getting his paws wet.

This continued all day long. Each time a duck fell, the dog walked across the surface of the water to retrieve it. The pessimist watched carefully but said nothing. Finally, on the drive home, Frank asked, "Did you notice anything unusual about my new dog?"

"Yes," said the pessimist. "He can't swim."

NOTES:
- This exercise is a good opportunity to review the "i" before "e" except after "c" rule.
- The story is full of run-on sentences. The correction above is, of course, only one of a number of ways to correct the piece.
- An appositive should be set off by commas. An appositive breaks the flow of the sentence to give more information about a noun. (Example: *He decided to introduce the dog first to a friend, an eternal pessimist who refused to be impressed by anything.*)
- When writing dialogue, start a new paragraph with each change of speakers.

Turtle

A little turtle began to climb a tree. It took him alot of time, but he finaly reached the top. He jumped into the air with excitement and then crashed to the ground. After catching his breathe he slowly climbed the tree again, jumped in the air, and fell to the ground.

The turtle repeated the same thing over and over again while a couple of birds sitting on a branch watched. Finaly, the female bird turned to her mate. "Dear," she said, "I think it may be time to tell him he's adopted."

POSSIBLE CORRECTION:

A little turtle began to climb a tree. It took him a lot of time, but he finally reached the top. He jumped into the air with excitement and then crashed to the ground. After catching his breath, he slowly climbed the tree again, jumped into the air, and fell to the ground.

The turtle repeated the same thing over and over again while a couple of birds sitting on a branch watched. Finally, the female bird turned to her mate. "Dear," she said, "I think it may be time to tell him he's adopted."

NOTES:
- *A lot* is two words, not one.
- *Breath* and *breathe* are often confused. *Breathe* is a verb, and *breath* is a noun.
- Introductory elements in a sentence should be followed by a comma. (Introductory elements include clauses, phrases, and introductory words like *yes, no, oh,* etc.)

Poor Baby Bear

A family of bears wound up in family court because of a divorce. Mama and Papa Bear were splitting up, and Baby Bear had to decide who he was going to live with.

The Judge asked, "Would you like to live with your father."

"Oh, no," said Baby Bear. "He beats me terribly."

"We can't have that, said the Judge. Let's have you live with your mother then.

"No way!" cried Baby Bear. "She beats me even worse than Papa!"

The Judge was quiet distresed. "You have to live with someone. Are there any relatives you would like to stay with."

"Yes, I'd like to live with my aunt Ethel Bear who lives in Chicago."

"Are you sure she will treat you well and not beat you?"

"Definitly," said Baby Bear. "The chicago bears never beat anybody."

POSSIBLE CORRECTION:

A family of bears wound up in family court because of a divorce. Mama and Papa Bear were splitting up, and Baby Bear had to decide who he was going to live with.

The judge asked, "Would you like to live with your father?"

"Oh, no," said Baby Bear. "He beats me terribly."

"We can't have that," said the judge. "Let's have you live with your mother then."

"No way!" cried Baby Bear. "She beats me even worse than Papa!"

The judge was quite distressed. "You have to live with someone. Are there any relatives you would like to stay with?"

"Yes, I'd like to live with my aunt Ethel Bear who lives in Chicago."

"Are you sure she will treat you well and not beat you?"

"Definitely," said Baby Bear. "The Chicago Bears never beat anybody."

NOTES:
- The word *judge* should not be capitalized unless it is used with the judge's name (*Judge Martinelli*).
- Use a question mark after a sentence that asks a question. If a quotation is a question, the question mark goes inside the quotation marks.

Hungry Roaches

Two roaches in boston massachusetts were munching on garbage in a alley when they started discusing a new restraunt across the Street.

"I was in that place," said one of the roaches. "Its amazingly clean. The floors shine, and the tables have freshly-washed tableclothes. The cupboards and counters are all scrubbed, and the kitchen is absolutly spotless."

"Please," said the other roach, frowning. "Not while I'm eating!"

POSSIBLE CORRECTION:

Two roaches in Boston, Massachusetts, were munching on garbage in an alley when they started discussing a new restaurant across the street.

"I was in that place," said one of the roaches. "It's amazingly clean. The floors shine, and the tables have freshly-washed tablecloths. The cupboards and counters are all scrubbed, and the kitchen is absolutely spotless."

"Please," said the other roach, frowning. "Not while I'm eating!"

NOTES:
- Separate city and state with a comma. Also use a comma *after* the state. (Many people forget the second comma.)
- Use *an* instead of *a* before a word with a vowel sound (*an alley*).
- There is no need to capitalize *street* unless it is used with the name of a specific street (*Elm Street, Claybourne Street*).

About the author

M.S. SAMSTON

M.S. Samston is a pseudonym for the staff writers at Cottonwood Press who worked together to create this book: Mary Gutting, Heather Madigan, Sarah Parman Stimely, Samantha Prust, and Cheryl Miller Thurston.

Exercise Title Index

Subject Index

More Great Books from Cottonwood Press

UNJOURNALING—Daily Writing exercises That Are NOT Personal, NOT Introspective, NOT Boring! The more than 200 impersonal but engaging writing prompts in this exercise book help students practice their writing skills without asking them to share personal thoughts they would rather keep to themselves.

A SENTENCE A DAY—Short, playful proofreading exercises to help students avoid tripping up when they write. This book focuses on short, playful, interesting sentences with a sense of humor.

ATTITUDE!—Helping students WANT to succeed in school and then setting them up for success. Pointing out what school has to do with real life, this easy-to-use book is enlightening and never preachy.

DOWNWRITE FUNNY—Using student's love of the ridiculous to build serious writing skills. The entertaining activities and illustrations in this book help teach all kinds of useful writing skills.

HOT FUDGE MONDAY—Tasty Ways to Teach Parts of Speech to Students Who Have a Hard Time Swallowing Anything To Do With Grammar. This new edition includes quirky quizzes, extended writing activities, and Internet enrichment activities that reinforce new skills.

THINKING IN THREES—The Power of Three in Writing. Faced with a writing task of any kind? Think of three things to say about the topic. Writing an essay? Remember that the body should have at least three paragraphs. Need help getting started? Learn three ways to begin an essay.

IF THEY'RE LAUGHING THEY JUST MIGHT BE LISTENING—Ideas for using HUMOR effectively in the classroom—even if you're NOT funny yourself. Discover ways to lighten up, encourage humor from others, and have fun with your students.

RELUCTANT DISCIPLINARIAN—Advice on classroom management from a softy who became (eventually) a successful teacher. Author Gary Rubinstein offers clear and specific advice for classroom management.

HOW TO HANDLE DIFFICULT PARENTS—A teacher's survival guide. Suzanne Capek Tingley identifies characteristics of some parent "types". She then goes on to give practical, easy-to-implement methods of working with them more effectively.

TWISTING ARMS—Teaching students how to write to persuade. This book is full of easy-to-use activities that will really sharpen students' writing and organizational skills.

COTTONWOODPRESS INC.
www.cottonwoodpress.com